Privacy Risk Analysis

Synthesis Lectures on Information Security, Privacy, & Trust

Editors
Elisa Bertino, *Purdue University*
Ravi Sandhu, *University of Texas, San Antonio*

The Synthesis Lectures Series on Information Security, Privacy, and Trust publishes 50- to 100-page publications on topics pertaining to all aspects of the theory and practice of Information Security, Privacy, and Trust. The scope largely follows the purview of premier computer security research journals such as ACM Transactions on Information and System Security, IEEE Transactions on Dependable and Secure Computing and Journal of Cryptology, and premier research conferences, such as ACM CCS, ACM SACMAT, ACM AsiaCCS, ACM CODASPY, IEEE Security and Privacy, IEEE Computer Security Foundations, ACSAC, ESORICS, Crypto, EuroCrypt and AsiaCrypt. In addition to the research topics typically covered in such journals and conferences, the series also solicits lectures on legal, policy, social, business, and economic issues addressed to a technical audience of scientists and engineers. Lectures on significant industry developments by leading practitioners are also solicited.

Privacy Risk Analysis
Sourya Joyee De and Daniel Le Métayer
2016

Introduction to Secure Outsourcing Computation
Xiaofeng Chen
2016

Database Anonymization: Privacy Models, Data Utility, and Microaggregation-based Inter-model Connections
Josep Domingo-Ferrer, David Sánchez, and Jordi Soria-Comas
2016

Automated Software Diversity
Per Larsen, Stefan Brunthaler, Lucas Davi, Ahmad-Reza Sadeghi, and Michael Franz
2015

Operating System Security
Trent Jaeger
2008

Privacy Risk Analysis

Sourya Joyee De and Daniel Le Métayer

ISBN: 978-3-031-01221-1   paperback
ISBN: 978-3-031-02349-1   ebook

DOI 10.1007/978-3-031-02349-1

A Publication in the Springer series
SYNTHESIS LECTURES ON INFORMATION SECURITY, PRIVACY, & TRUST

Lecture #17
Series Editors: Elisa Bertino, *Purdue University*
                Ravi Sandhu, *University of Texas, San Antonio*
Series ISSN
Print 1945-9742   Electronic 1945-9750

Privacy Risk Analysis

Sourya Joyee De and Daniel Le Métayer
Inria, Université de Lyon

*SYNTHESIS LECTURES ON INFORMATION SECURITY, PRIVACY, &
TRUST #17*

ABSTRACT

Privacy Risk Analysis fills a gap in the existing literature by providing an introduction to the basic notions, requirements, and main steps of conducting a privacy risk analysis.

The deployment of new information technologies can lead to significant privacy risks and a privacy impact assessment should be conducted before designing a product or system that processes personal data. However, if existing privacy impact assessment frameworks and guidelines provide a good deal of details on organizational aspects (including budget allocation, resource allocation, stakeholder consultation, etc.), they are much vaguer on the technical part, in particular on the actual risk assessment task. For privacy impact assessments to keep up their promises and really play a decisive role in enhancing privacy protection, they should be more precise with regard to these technical aspects.

This book is an excellent resource for anyone developing and/or currently running a risk analysis as it defines the notions of personal data, stakeholders, risk sources, feared events, and privacy harms all while showing how these notions are used in the risk analysis process. It includes a running smart grids example to illustrate all the notions discussed in the book.

KEYWORDS

privacy, personal data, data protection, risk, analysis, impact, harm, vulnerability, countermeasure, anonymization, law, legal, regulation

Contents

Preface

Risk analysis and risk management are common approaches in areas as varied as environment protection, public health and computer security. In some sense, one may also argue that the original purpose of data protection laws was to reduce the risks to privacy posed by the development of new technologies [58]. In Europe however, the current Data Protection Directive [47] does not rely heavily on privacy risk analysis or Privacy Impact Assessment (PIA).[1] The situation is going to change dramatically with the new General Data Protection Regulation (GDPR) [48], which shall apply from May 25, 2018.

The GDPR represents a fundamental shift from an administrative process based on *a priori* controls to a risk-based accountability approach in which PIAs[2] play a key role. The virtues of the risk-based approach to privacy have been praised by many authors and stakeholders [26]. The main practical benefit expected from the approach is an increased effectiveness in terms of privacy protection: risk assessment makes it possible to focus on the most significant problems and to calibrate measures based on the estimated risks. Organizations also appreciate the fact that legal requirements can be implemented with greater flexibility. Another argument in favor of the risk-based approach is the observation that it is more and more difficult to draw a clear line between anonymous data and personal data, or between sensitive data and non-sensitive data. For this reason, there is a growing view that the only way forward is to go beyond dual visions in this matter and to rely on assessments of actual risks rather than fixed definitions and obligations [120, 128].

However more nuanced views have also been expressed on this topic. For example, the Working Party 29 [6] stresses that the risk-based approach should never lead to a weakening of the rights of the individuals: the rights granted to the data subject should be respected regardless of the level of risk (right of access, erasure, objection, etc.). The fundamental principles applicable to data controllers should also remain the same (legitimacy, data minimization, purpose limitation, transparency, data integrity, etc.), even if they can be scalable (based on the results of a risk assessment). In addition, the risk-based approach should consider not only harms to individuals but also general societal impacts.

Some privacy advocates also fear that the flexibility provided by the risk-based approach is abused by some organizations, and risk assessment is perverted into a self-legitimation exercise [57]. To avoid this drift and ensure that the risk-based approach really contributes to improving privacy, a number of conditions have to be met. First and foremost, the analysis has to be rigorous, both from the technical point of view and from the procedural point of view. The

---

[1]The notion is even not referred to explicitly in the text of the Directive.
[2]More precisely, the GDPR uses the wording "Data Protection Impact Assessment."

methodology used for the analysis should be clearly defined, as well as the assumptions about the context and the potential privacy impacts. This is a key requirement to ensure that the results of a privacy risk analysis are trustworthy and can be subject to independent checks.

However, if existing PIA frameworks and guidelines [160, 161, 163] provide a good deal of details on organizational aspects (including budget allocation, resource allocation, stakeholder consultation, etc.), they are much vaguer on the technical part, in particular on the actual risk assessment task.

A key step to achieve a better convergence between PIA frameworks geared toward legal and organizational issues on one hand and technical approaches to privacy risk analysis on the other hand, is to agree on a common terminology and a set of basic notions. It is also necessary to characterize the main tasks to be carried out in a privacy risk analysis and their inputs and outputs.

The above objectives are precisely the subject of this book. The intended audience includes both computer scientists looking for an introductory survey on privacy risk analysis and stakeholders involved in a PIA process with the desire to address technical aspects in a rigorous way. We hope that the reader will have as much pleasure in reading this book as we had in putting it together.

Sourya Joyee De and Daniel Le Métayer
August 2016

Acknowledgments

We thank our colleagues of the PRIVATICS research group in Grenoble and Lyon, in particular Gergely Ács and Claude Castelluccia for their comments on an earlier draft of this book and many fruitful discussions on privacy risk analysis. This work has been partially funded by the French ANR-12-INSE-0013 project BIOPRIV and the Inria Project Lab CAPPRIS.

Sourya Joyee De and Daniel Le Métayer
August 2016

CHAPTER 1

Introduction

Considering that the deployment of new information technologies can lead to substantial privacy risks for individuals, there is a growing recognition that a privacy impact assessment (PIA) should be conducted before the design of a product collecting or processing personal data. De facto PIAs have become more and more popular during the last decade. Several countries such as Australia, New Zealand, Canada, the U.S. and the United Kingdom [164] have played a leading role in this movement. Europe has also promoted PIAs in areas such as RFIDs [9, 107] and smart grids [11, 12] and is putting strong emphasis on privacy and data protection risk analysis in its new General Data Protection Regulation (GDPR)[1] [48]. However, if existing PIA frameworks and guidelines provide a good deal of details on organizational aspects (including budget allocation, resource allocation, stakeholder consultation, etc.), they are much vaguer on the technical part (what we call "Privacy Risk Analysis" or "PRA" in this book), in particular on the actual risk assessment task. Some tools have also been proposed to help in the management of organizational aspects [3, 118, 144] but no support currently exists to perform the technical analysis. For PIAs to keep up their promises and really play a decisive role to enhance privacy protection, they should be more precise with regard to these technical aspects. This is a key requirement to ensure that their results are trustworthy and can be subject to independent checks. However, this is also a challenge because privacy is a multifaceted notion involving a wide variety of factors that may be difficult to assess.

Some work has already been carried out on PRA in the computer science community [39, 40, 52, 169] but the results of these efforts are not yet integrated within existing PIA frameworks. A first step to achieve a better convergence between PIA frameworks geared toward legal and organizational issues on one hand and technical approaches to PRA on the other hand, is to agree on a common terminology and a set of basic notions. It is also necessary to characterize the main tasks to be carried out in a privacy risk analysis and their inputs and outputs.

Surveys of current practices and recommendations have already been published for PIAs [29, 160, 163, 164] but, as far as we know, not for PRAs. The goal of this book is to fill this gap by providing an introduction to the basic notions, requirements and key steps of a privacy risk analysis. Apart from Chapter 9, in which we put PRA into the context of PIA, we focus on the technical part of the process here. For example, we do not consider legal obligations such as the obligation to notify the supervisory authority before carrying out personal data processing (in

---

[1]Conducting a PIA will become mandatory for certain categories of personal data processing.

European jurisdictions). Neither do we discuss the organization of the stakeholders consultation which forms an integral part of a PIA.

Another choice made in this book is to focus on privacy risks for persons (including individuals, groups and society as a whole) who have to suffer from privacy violations rather than the risks for organizations processing the data (data controllers or data processors in the European terminology). Certain frameworks [55, 106, 107] integrate both types of risks but we believe that this can be a source of confusion because, even if they are interrelated, these risks concern two types of stakeholders with different, and sometimes conflicting, interests. The risks to business, or to organizations in general, posed by privacy can be analyzed in a second stage, when privacy risks for persons have been evaluated, since the former can be seen as indirect consequences of the latter.

Chapter 2 sets the scene with a review of the common terms used in privacy risk analysis, a study of their variations and a definition of the terminology used in this book. We proceed with detailed presentations of the components of a privacy risk analysis and suggestions of classifications, considering successively, processing systems (Chapter 3), personal data (Chapter 4), stakeholders (Chapter 5), risk sources (Chapter 6), feared events (Chapter 7) and privacy harms (Chapter 8). Then, we show how all the notions introduced in this book can be used in a privacy risk analysis process (Chapter 9). We conclude with a reflection on security and privacy risk analysis and avenues for further work (Chapter 10).

We use a running example in the area of smart grids (the BEMS System introduced in Chapter 3) to illustrate all the notions discussed in this book.

CHAPTER 2

Terminology

Before getting into the substance of the matter, it is necessary to define precisely the main concepts involved in a privacy risk analysis. Indeed, technical terms are not always used in a consistent way in this area and different authors sometimes use the same words with different meanings. The objective of this chapter is to set the scene and introduce the terminology used throughout this book.

In the following subsections, we define successively the notions of:

1. *personal data*, which is the object of protection;

2. *stakeholders*, which relate to or handle personal data at various stages of their lifecycle;

3. *risk sources*, which may cause privacy breaches;

4. *feared events*, which may lead to privacy harms; and

5. *privacy harms*, which are the impacts of privacy breaches on individuals, groups of individuals or society as a whole.

Some of these notions, such as privacy harms, have been extensively discussed by legal scholars even though they have received less attention from law makers. Others, such as personal data, are defined by privacy laws and regulations. Still others, such as feared events, have been used only by certain data protection authorities. However, even for terms that are well-discussed, there is generally no single interpretation of their meaning. Therefore, in the following sections we provide a concise definition of each of these terms (which will be further discussed in the next chapters). For some of them, we agree with one of the existing definitions, while for others we provide our own and justify our choice. In the rest of the book, unless otherwise mentioned, these terms will be used in the sense defined in this chapter.

2.1 PERSONAL DATA

Both the European Union (EU) and the United States (U.S.) privacy regulations rely on notions of "data" or "information" but they follow different approaches. While the EU defines the notion of "personal data," the U.S. refers to "personally identifiable information" (or "PII"). The use of these terms reveals substantial differences in the ways of considering privacy on each side of the Atlantic.

The notion of personal data used in this book is mainly inspired by the definitions provided by the EU Data Protection Directive ("EU Directive" in the sequel) [47] and the EU General Data Protection Regulation ("GDPR" in the sequel) [48]. The primary reason for this choice is that the EU provides a single, uniform definition, which contrasts with the multiple, competing attempts at defining PII in the U.S. [134, 135].

Article 4(1) of the GDPR [48] defines personal data as follows:

"'Personal data' means any information relating to an identified or identifiable natural person ('data subject'); an identifiable person is one who can be identified, directly or indirectly, in particular by reference to an identifier such as a name, an identification number, location data, an online identifier or to one or more factors specific to the physical, physiological, genetic, mental, economic, cultural or social identity of that natural person."

The GDPR (Recital 26) adds a clarification about pseudonymization and identification: *"Personal data which has undergone pseudonymisation, which could be attributed to a natural person by the use of additional information, should be considered to be information on an identifiable natural person. To determine whether a natural person is identifiable, account should be taken of all the means reasonably likely to be used, such as singling out, either by the controller or by another person to identify the natural person directly or indirectly."*

This position is inspired by the Working Party 29.[1] Opinion 08/2012 [10] suggesting that *"any information allowing a natural person to be singled out and treated differently"* should be considered as personal data. Our definition of personal data is in line with the approaches followed by the GDPR and the Working Party 29.

Definition 2.1   Personal Data [10, 47, 48].   Personal data is any information relating to an identified or identifiable natural person[2] and any information allowing such a person to be singled out or treated differently.

Considering the fact that a person can be singled out or treated differently makes it possible to take into account data processing that can have privacy impacts, such as discriminatory treatments (e.g., discriminatory ads [38]), without necessarily identifying any individual.

The different approaches followed for the definition of personal data in the EU and the U.S. are further discussed in Chapter 4.

2.2   STAKEHOLDERS

The term "stakeholder" is commonly used in the literature, generally without definition. Even though its meaning may look obvious, we define it as follows to avoid any ambiguity.

---

[1]The Working Party 29, or Article 29 Working Party, is a group set up under the EU Directive. It includes a representative from each European data protection authority. One of its missions is to provide recommendations to the European Commission and to the public with regard to data protection and the implementation of the EU Directive.
[2]This person is the "data subject" defined in Definition 2.2.

Definition 2.2   Stakeholder.   A stakeholder is any entity (individual or organization) to which a piece of data relates or that processes[3] or gets access (legally or not) to a piece of data at any stage of its lifecycle.

The EU Directive provides comprehensive definitions of different types of stakeholders, whereas the U.S. privacy laws and regulations rely on sectoral definitions. In this book, we follow the same approach as the EU Directive and consider the following stakeholders:

- data controllers,

- data subjects,

- data processors and

- third parties.

We also chose to use definitions inspired by the EU Directive for these terms.

Definition 2.3   Data Subject [10, 32, 47, 48].   A data subject is an identified or identifiable natural person whom the personal data relates to.

Definition 2.4   Data Controller [32, 47].   A data controller is an entity (individual or organization) that, alone or jointly with others, determines the purpose, conditions and means of processing of personal data.

Definition 2.5   Data Processor [47].   A data processor is an entity (individual or organization) that processes personal data on behalf of the data controller.

Definition 2.6   Third Party [47].   A third party is an entity (individual or organization) other than the data subject, the controller, the processor and the persons who, under the direct authority of the controller or the processor, are authorized to process the data.

Typical examples of third parties include ad brokers installing cookies on the computer of the data subject, marketing companies receiving personal data from the data controller, or pairs in a social network.

Some difficulties may arise while applying these definitions in practical scenarios, especially those that involve multi-party processing arrangements and cloud computing. In some cases, the notion of the data controller and the data processor cannot be distinguished very easily.[4]

The roles defined above are not mutually exclusive. For example, a data controller for one set of data or operations may act as a data processor for another set of data or operations. Moreover,

---

[3]Here we define "processing" in the same way as in the EU Directive as *"any operation or set of operations which is performed upon personal data, whether or not by automatic means, such as collection, recording, organization, storage, adaptation or alteration, retrieval, consultation, use, disclosure by transmission, dissemination or otherwise making available, alignment or combination, block-ing, erasure or destruction."*

[4]This issue is further discussed in Section 5.1.

consistently with the approach followed in the EU Directive, the above definitions do not imply the lawfulness of the actions of any entity. A data controller, for example, may legally or illegally process data; it may process data without any legitimate purpose or collect more data than necessary for the purpose. This is in agreement with the opinion of the Working Party 29 [8] clarifying that the data controller only "determines" rather than "lawfully determines" the purpose and the means for data processing.

2.3 RISK SOURCES

One of the first steps in a risk analysis is to identify the potential sources of risks, that is to say the entities whose actions can lead to a privacy breach. These entities are often referred to as "adversaries" or "attackers" in the security literature but we prefer to use the term "risk source" here as it is less security-laden and it is not limited to malicious actors. We define a risk source as follows:

Definition 2.7 Risk source. A risk source is any entity (individual or organization) that may process (legally or illegally) personal data related to a data subject and whose actions may directly or indirectly, intentionally or unintentionally lead to privacy harms.

Any of the stakeholders, apart from the data subject himself,[5] may be a risk source. Each risk source should be associated with a number of attributes, including its capabilities, background information, motivations, etc. We discuss risk sources and their attributes in Chapter 6.

2.4 FEARED EVENTS

A feared event is a technical event in the processing system that can lead to a privacy harm. An unauthorized party getting access to the health data of a patient or a controller re-identifying a person from an alleged anonymized dataset are examples of feared events. The occurrence of a feared event depends on the existence of weaknesses (of the system or the organization), which we call privacy weaknesses, and the ability of the risk sources to exploit them.

Definition 2.8 Feared Event. A feared event is an event of the processing system that may lead to a privacy harm.

Definition 2.9 Privacy weakness. A privacy weakness is a weakness in the data protection mechanisms (whether technical, organizational or legal) of a system or lack thereof.

As an illustration, a weak encryption algorithm used to protect personal data is a privacy weakness. Weak anonymization algorithms are other examples of privacy weaknesses. The term "vulnerability" is often used with a close meaning in the area of computer security, but we choose the expression "privacy weakness" here because in some cases privacy harms can stem from the

---

[5]However, a data subject may act as a risk source for another data subject.

functionality of the system itself[6] (which would probably not be considered as a vulnerability in the usual sense of the word). For the same reason, we use the expression "harm scenario" to denote the succession of events leading to a feared event, which is often referred to as an "attack" in the security literature. In the simplest cases (for example an unauthorized employee getting access to unprotected data), the exploitation of the privacy weakness is the feared event itself and the harm scenario boils down to a single event. A more complex harm scenario would be a succession of access attempts using passwords from a dictionary and leading to the discovery of the correct password and the access to the personal data.

Definition 2.10 Harm scenario.   A harm scenario is a succession of events or actions leading to a feared event.

2.5   PRIVACY HARMS

Feared events denote events (in a technical sense) that have to be avoided. The ultimate goal of a privacy risk analysis is the study of the impacts of these events on individuals, groups or society, which we call the "privacy harms." For instance, the unauthorized access to health data (a feared event) by a risk source may cause privacy harms such as discrimination (against a patient or a group of patients) or psychological distress. Similarly, the illegal access to location data such as home address may lead to economic or physical injury (e.g., burglary or murder[7]).

The characterization of privacy harms is not an easy task as it may depend on many contextual factors (cultural, social, personal, etc.). Obviously, societies in different parts of the world follow different sets of unwritten rules and norms of behavior. For example, a data subject belonging to a certain society may feel uneasy if his religious beliefs (or lack thereof) or sexual preferences are revealed. "Acceptance in society" is generally an important factor for individual well-being and should be considered in the risk analysis.

The definition of privacy harms adopted in this book is inspired by Solove's vivid description of how feared events may affect individuals and society as a whole [140]. It also bears close similarities with the definition of harms proposed by Center for Information Policy Leadership (CIPL) [26].

Definition 2.11 Privacy Harms.   Privacy harm is a negative impact of the use of a processing system on a data subject, or a group of data subjects, or society as a whole, from the standpoint of physical, mental, or financial well-being or reputation, dignity, freedom, acceptance in society, self-actualization, domestic life, freedom of expression or any fundamental right.

The above definition takes into consideration the impact on society, because certain harms, like surveillance, are bound to have global impacts such as chilling effect or loss of creativity which

---

[6]For example, in the case of video-surveillance systems or location-based services.
[7]This happened for example in the case of the murder of actress Rebecca Schaeffer in 1989 where the murderer extracted her home address from the Department of Motor Vehicle records [104, 140].

are matters for all society, not just individuals. As discussed in Chapter 1, this definition of privacy harms does not concern the impacts on the data controllers or the data processors themselves, which could be considered in a second stage (as indirect consequences of privacy harms) but are not included in the scope of this book.[8]

2.6 PRIVACY RISKS

The word "risk" is used in this book (as often in the risk management literature) as a contraction of "level of risk." Levels of risk are generally defined by two values [17, 32, 55]: likelihood and severity.[9]

The GDPR also refers explicitly to these two dimensions in its Recital 76:

"The likelihood and severity of the risk to the rights and freedoms of the data subject should be determined by reference to the nature, scope, context and purposes of the processing. Risk should be evaluated on the basis of an objective assessment, by which it is established whether data processing operations involve a risk or a high risk."

In the context of privacy, the likelihood characterizes the probability that a privacy harm may be caused by the processing system, and the severity represents the magnitude of the impact on the victims. The likelihood should combine the probabilities that a risk source will initiate a harm scenario, the probability that it will be able to carry out the necessary tasks (i.e., perform the scenario, including the exploitation of the privacy weaknesses of the system, to bring about a feared event) and the probability that the feared event will cause a harm [17]. The likelihood and the severity can be defined in a quantitative or qualitative manner (for example, using a fixed scale such as "low," "medium," "high"). Risks are often pictured in two dimensional spaces [33] or matrices [17]. They are also sometimes reduced to a single value through the use of rules to calculate products of likelihoods by impacts [55].

2.7 PRIVACY RISK ANALYSIS

The first goals of a privacy risk analysis are the identification of the privacy harms that may result from the use of the processing system and the assessment of their severity and likelihood. Based on this analysis, decision makers and experts can then decide which risks are not acceptable and select appropriate measures[10] to address them. The risk analysis can be iterated to ensure that the risks have been reduced to an acceptable level. Considering that risk analyses always rely on certain assumptions (e.g., about the state-of-the art of the technology or the motivations of the potential risk sources), they should be maintained and repeated on a regular basis. Among the challenges facing the analyst, particular attention must be paid to two main difficulties:

---

[8]This phase can typically take the form of a more traditional risk/benefit analysis considering the potential consequences of privacy harms for the controller (mostly in financial, reputational and legal terms).

[9]The severity is sometimes called the "impact" or "adverse impact" [17, 55].

[10]In general, the decision can be to accept a risk, to avoid or mitigate it, or to share or transfer it. Mitigation or avoidance measures can be combinations of technical, organizational and legal controls.

1. the consideration of all factors that can have an impact on privacy risks and

2. the appropriate assessment of these impacts and their contribution to the assessment of the overall risks.

To discuss these issues in a systematic way, we propose in the next chapters a collection of six components (respectively: processing system, personal data, stakeholders, risk sources, feared events and privacy harms), each of them being associated with:

1. *categories* of elements to be considered for the component[11] and

2. *attributes* which have to be defined and taken into account for the evaluation of the risks.[12]

Even though they are not necessarily comprehensive, categories are useful to minimize the risks of omission during the analysis. They take the form of catalogues, typologies or knowledge bases in existing methodologies [33, 55]. For their part, attributes help analysts identify all relevant factors for each component. The use of templates in certain methodologies [33] fulfill a similar role. Table A.1 in Appendix A provides a summary of the categories and the attributes suggested for each component.

---

[11]For example, the categories of data being processed by a health information system may include health data, contact data, identification data, genetic data, etc.

[12]For example, the level of motivation of a risk source or the level of precision of location data.

CHAPTER 3

Processing System

The first step of a privacy risk analysis is the definition of its scope, which requires a detailed and comprehensive description of the processing system under consideration. This description should include all personal data flows between the components of the system and communications with the outside world. This information is necessary for the privacy risk analysis, in particular for the identification of the privacy weaknesses and the capacities of the risk sources to get access to the personal data.

To summarize, the description should be sufficient to ensure that all potential privacy problems arising out of the system can be detected [106]. In most cases (at least for systems developed following a rigorous methodology), a detailed documentation about the system should already be available and it should be sufficient to supplement it with some additional information to meet the requirements of a privacy risk analysis.

In this chapter, we present a set of attributes useful to characterize a processing system with a view to privacy risk analysis (Section 3.1) and introduce the running example used throughout this book (the BEMS System) with its attributes (Section 3.2).

3.1 SYSTEM ATTRIBUTES

In order to meet the needs of the subsequent steps of the privacy risk analysis, the description of the system should include at least the following attributes:

1. The *functional specification* describing the functionalities that the system is supposed to provide, including the potential use cases or scenarios. The functional specification should be consistent with the declared purpose of the system. It is also useful during the analysis to check compliance with the data minimization principle (personal data should be collected only if necessary to achieve the purpose).

2. The *controls* including all existing measures (technical and organizational) to protect personal data. Precise knowledge of existing controls is necessary to detect potential privacy weaknesses.

3. The *interface* including all interactions of the system with the external world, including users and other systems, and the possibility or not to collect the consent of the user. The interface is useful, inter alia, to detect potential risks related to data dissemination, transfers to third parties and lack of control from the users.

4. The *data flows* describing the internal view of the system, including the basic components, their locations, supporting assets, the access rights and the data flows between them. The analysis of the data flows is instrumental in the search for privacy weaknesses.

5. The *supporting assets* consisting of all software, hardware and networks on which the system relies and the stakeholders controlling them. Supporting assets, in conjunction with data flows and actors, are useful to analyze the capacities of the risk sources to get access to personal data.

6. The *actors* having access to the system or interacting with it, including roles inside the organization of the data controller and the access rights of each actor.

This set of attributes is inspired by previous work on privacy risk analysis. For example, the view-based approach proposed by Oetzel and Spiekermann [106] includes:

1. The *system view*, which takes into account applications, system components, hardware, software, interfaces and the network topology.

2. The *functional view*, which consists of generic business processes, use cases, technical controls, roles and users.

3. The *data view*, which consists of categories of data processed by the system, data flow diagrams, actors and data types.

4. The *physical environment view*, which includes physical security and operational controls such as backup and contingency measures.

A whole chapter (Chapter 4) is dedicated to personal data in this book. The other components presented in [106] overlap with the above list of attributes.

The definition of the data flows is a key part of the characterization of a system. A standard approach is to resort to *data flow diagrams (DFD)*, which are structured, graphical representations based on four main types of building blocks: external entities, data stores, data flows and processes [166]. Deng et al. [40] propose an enhanced representation of data flows with trust boundaries to separate trustworthy and untrustworthy elements of the system. These boundaries are used to identify the potential risk sources. As argued in [166], the definition of the DFD is a crucial step in a privacy risk analysis and an incorrect DFD is likely to result in erroneous conclusions about privacy risks. Moreover, the granularity of the DFD dictates the level of detail at which the analysis can be conducted.

3.2 ILLUSTRATION: THE BEMS SYSTEM

In this section, we introduce the BEMS[1] System used to illustrate the concepts discussed throughout this book. The BEMS System includes the billing and the energy management functionalities

---

[1]Billing and Energy Management System.

of a hypothetical smart grid system. This choice is not insignificant: smart grid initiatives, which are now under deployment in many countries, already face a large number of privacy related questions. As utility providers promise benefits in terms of home energy management, researchers [20, 36, 64, 88, 95, 98, 122, 159] warn against the potential privacy harms posed by the collection of highly granular energy consumption data. Many potential privacy harms of various levels of likelihood and severity have already been identified, including surveillance by governments and law enforcing bodies [25, 43, 88, 94, 96], burglary [88, 94, 122] and targeted advertising [19, 25, 88, 93, 94, 122]. Utility providers are facing the task of taking appropriate measures and convincing both their consumers and regulatory bodies that these measures are sufficient to handle potential harms. Carrying out privacy impact assessments is therefore inevitable for the smart grid industry [36]. Needless to say, our goal is not to provide a full scale privacy risk analysis for a smart grid system here but, more modestly, to use some of its features as a working example to illustrate the notions presented in this book.

The system attributes introduced in the previous section are defined as follows for the BEMS System:

1. *Functional specification.*

    - The *User Registration System* is used to register new consumers with the utility provider.
    - The *Consumer Information System* stores and manages all consumer identification, contact, billing and energy management information. It consists of the Consumer Data Store and the Consumer Information Management Application. The latter implements security functions for the protection of the Consumer Data Store. In particular, it is involved in ensuring that only authorized applications, sub-systems and actors get access to the data. It also performs other functions such as the creation of the meter ID and the user portal account number.
    - The *Meter Data Management System* stores and manages the energy consumption data and the corresponding meter ID. It consists of the Meter Data Store and the Meter Data Management Application. The Meter Data Management Application ensures that only authorized sub-systems, applications and actors can access the data and implements other security-related functions to ensure the protection of the Meter Data Store.
    - The *Utility Gateway* collects energy consumption data (corresponding to meter IDs) from smart meters. It contributes to the implementation of some functionalities of the Meter Data Management Application by ensuring that only the authorized sub-systems, applications and actors can access the data.
    - The *Smart Meter* collects energy consumption data from home appliances. It includes a security module to encrypt and sign the data before sending it to the utility gateway.
    - The *Payment Management System* handles all billing, payment and energy management related functions. It consists of three applications: the Billing Application that

generates the bills, the Energy Management Application that generates the energy management suggestions and the Payment Application that updates the payment status for each consumer.

- The *Price Determination System* computes the fees for the different time periods of the billing cycle.

- The *User Interface* is used by the consumers to get access to their bills and the energy management suggestions as well as to update or correct any identification or contact information whenever necessary.

Table 3.2 defines all the abbreviations for the BEMS sub-systems used in this book.

2. *Interfaces.* The interactions with the consumer take place through the User Interface component. The Smart Meter collects the energy consumption data from the home appliances. The Payment Application interacts with the bank to receive information about payments.

3. *Data flows.* The data flows between the main components of the system are depicted in Fig. 3.1. The Smart Meter and the Utility Gateway are located in the consumers' premises. The User Interface can be accessed by the consumer through the Internet from his PC. All other systems are located with the utility provider and cannot be accessed by the consumer.

Each new consumer registers with the utility provider using the User Registration System by providing his identification and contact details. The User Registration System transfers this information to the Consumer Information System which creates a meter ID and a user portal account number for each new registered user.

Within the consumer premises, energy consumption data from home appliances are collected by the smart meter. This communication is based on the Zigbee standard. The smart meter then transfers this data to the utility gateway, along with the meter ID, every 15 minutes. The utility gateway gathers data from several smart meters. These data are then transferred to the utility provider to be stored and managed by the Meter Data Management System.

During each billing cycle,[2] the Payment Management System accesses the energy consumption data for each meter ID from the Meter Data Management System and the tariffs per time period from the Price Determination System. The Billing Application within the Payment Management System computes the bills associated with each meter ID, whereas the Energy Management Application creates the energy management suggestions based on the bills and the energy consumption data during each billing cycle. The Payment Application within the Payment Management System updates the payment status for each meter ID based on the bills and the payment information received from the bank, corresponding to the bank account number obtained from the Consumer Information System. The

---

[2]The billing cycle, which is generally one month, is defined by the utility provider.

Table 3.1: Supporting assets

Types of Supporting Assets	Examples
Hardware	One database server, application server, load balancers, clients (PC, notebook, tablet, mobile phone, printer etc.), storage media (semiconductor, optical, paper), network components (switch, router, bridge, gateway, firewall, modem), smart meter, security module
Applications	Billing Application, Energy Management Application, Meter Data Management Application, Consumer Information Management Application, Payment Application
Data stores	Meter Data Store, Consumer Data Store
Software environment	Standard software, operating systems, device driver, firmware, services (mail, file etc.)

Table 3.2: List of abbreviations

Abbreviation	Meaning
URS	User Registration System
CIS	Consumer Information System
MDMS	Meter Data Management System
UG	Utility Gateway
SM	Smart Meter
PMS	Payment Management System
PDS	Price Determination System
UI	User Interface
BA	Billing Application
EMA	Energy Management Application
MDMA	Meter Data Management Application
CIMA	Consumer Information Management Application
PA	Payment Application
MDS	Meter Data Store
CDS	Consumer Data Store

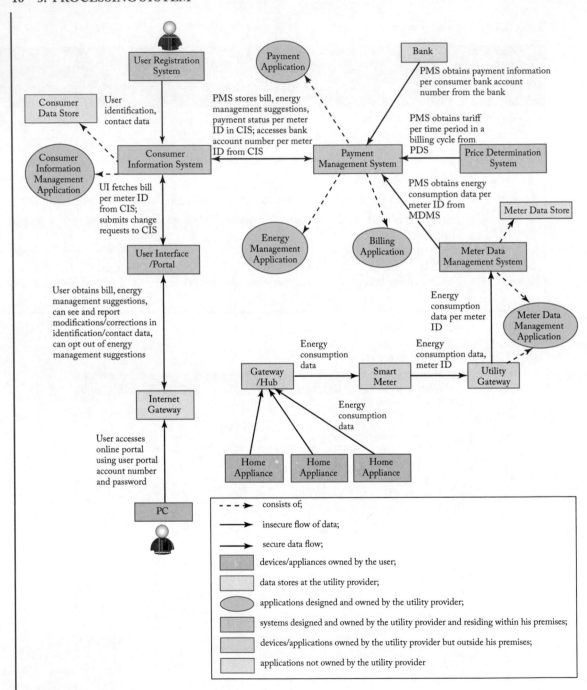

Figure 3.1: BEMS data flow diagram.

resulting bill, the energy management suggestions and the payment status per meter ID are transferred to the Consumer Information System for storage.

Each consumer, using his user portal account number, can access the User Interface. The User Interface fetches from the Consumer Information System the bill and energy management suggestions corresponding to his meter ID. The User Interface also displays the contact and the identification details to the user. The user can request updates or corrections of the identification and the contact details through the User Interface.

All the data are stored and transferred encrypted and signed, with the exception of the transfer of the energy consumption data from the home appliances to the smart meter, which is not fully secure.[3]

4. *Supporting assets.* The supporting assets are defined in Table 3.1.

5. *Actors.* The actors of the BEMS System are the following: consumers, system administrators, service technicians (for installation and maintenance of smart meters and utility gateways), developers, operators and other employees under the utility provider.

---

[3]Various security vulnerabilities of the Zigbee standard are documented in [155, 170].

CHAPTER 4

Personal Data

In this chapter, we first discuss the differences between the definitions of personally identifiable information (PII) in the U.S. and personal data in Europe (Section 4.1). We also summarize the ongoing debates on anonymization which is a central issue in this context (Section 4.2). We proceed with a categorization of personal data and a discussion about specific categories of data considered sensitive by certain regulations (Section 4.3). Next, we present the set of data attributes to be considered in a privacy risk analysis (Section 4.4). Data categories and attributes are then illustrated with the BEMS System (Section 4.5).

4.1 EUROPEAN AND U.S. VIEWS

The notions of "personal data" in the EU and "personally identifiable information" (PII) in the U.S., which are the cornerstones of modern privacy regulations, do not carry exactly the same meaning. The first part of our discussion concentrates on these variations and the differences between the U.S. and the EU approaches to privacy.

Table B.1 in Appendix B shows various definitions of personal data and personally identifiable information. The sources of these definitions are mostly privacy laws and standardization documents. For example, the CNIL[1] guidelines [32, 33] refer to the definitions of personal data from the EU Directive [47], the French Data Protection Act [50] and the ISO standard ISO/IEC 29100:2011 [72].

Considering the central role of the notion of personal data in the legal framework, the EU Directive [47] has introduced the following general definition:

"Personal data shall mean any information relating to an identified or identifiable natural person ("data subject"); an identifiable person is one who can be identified, directly or indirectly, in particular by reference to an identification number or to one or more factors specific to his physical, physiological, mental, economic, cultural or social identity."

As a first comment, it may be noted that the EU Directive does not seem to make a difference between "data" and "information." In fact, the two words are not always used with the same meaning in the literature[2] but this distinction is not essential here and we will, as the EU Directive, use them interchangeably

---

[1]The CNIL ("Commission Nationale de l'Informatique et des Libertés") is the French Data Protection Authority.

[2]See, for example, the Wikipedia definition of data: *"Data becomes information by interpretation; e.g., the height of Mt. Everest is generally considered data, a book on Mt. Everest geological characteristics may be considered information, and a report containing practical information on the best way to reach Mt. Everest's peak may be considered knowledge."*

According to the Working Party 29 [7], an identifiable person within a group is a person who can be distinguished from the others in the group.[3] As discussed in Chapter 2, the GDPR and our definition are in line with this position. Under the German law, Dammann [37] interprets it in a more restricted sense, as follows: *"A person is identified when it is clear that the data relate to the person and not to another."* In the context of the United Kingdom, Jay [75] states that *"A person becomes identified where there is sufficient information either to contact him or to recognize him by picking him out in some way from others and know who he/she is,"* which seems also to be more restrictive than the Working Party 29's definition since it implies that the person can be reached, whereas the Working Party 29 refers only to distinguishability.

Unlike the EU Directive, the U.S. laws and regulations have not really tried to define personally identifiable information in a general way. The three predominant approaches in the U.S. in this regard have been [134, 135]:

1. *The tautological approach.* PII is sometimes defined simply as any information identifying a person. The Video Privacy Protection Act (VPPA) is an example of this approach (see Table B.1 in Appendix B).

2. *The non-public approach.* Another option is to try to outline what personal information *is not* rather than what it is. For example, the Gramm-Leach-Bliley Act (see Table B.1 in Appendix B) states that any publicly accessible or purely statistical information is outside its scope.

3. *The closed list approach.* Under this approach, information is qualified as personal if it falls within an enumerated list of categories. For example, the Massachusetts breach notification statute requires that individuals be notified if there is a loss or a leakage of specific types of personal information. They include the first name or first initial and the last name of a Massachusetts resident in combination with one or more of the following: 1) social security number, 2) driver's license number or state-issued identification card number and 3) financial account number or credit/debit card number with or without any required security code, access code, personal identification number or password that would permit access to a resident's financial account [111].

None of the above approaches actually defines what is meant by personally identifiable information. The tautological approach is self-referential. The non-public approach, instead of trying to determine whether a piece of information is identifiable, focuses on a different issue: whether the data has been disclosed or not. The closed list approach may be sufficient in certain contexts but it is restrictive and it does not provide any general method for distinguishing a PII from a non-PII.

---

[3]*"As regards "indirectly" identified or identifiable persons, this category typically relates to the phenomenon of "unique combinations," whether small or large in size. In cases where prima facie the extent of the identifiers available does not allow anyone to single out a particular person, that person might still be "identifiable" because that information combined with other pieces of information (whether the latter is retained by the data controller or not) will allow the individual to be distinguished from others."* [7]

Table B.1 in Appendix B shows the differences between the EU and the U.S. views on data. These differences have also been discussed at length by Schwartz and Solove [135]. Most of them seem to result from deeper differences in the ways privacy itself is considered in the EU and in the U.S. Basically, in the EU, privacy is looked upon as a fundamental right[4] whereas the U.S. treats it as one of many concerns, often secondary to others such as freedom of speech or economic development. It is significant in this respect that the most influential agency in the field of privacy in the U.S. is the Federal Trade Commission whereas the relevant authorities in Europe are the Data Protection Authorities. This discussion, which involves complex legal, philosophical, cultural and historical considerations, goes beyond the scope of this book.

4.2   IDENTIFIABILITY AND ANONYMIZATION

At the core of the definitions of personal data and PII lies the term "identifiability." However, there are differing opinions about what should be considered "identifiable" information. Moreover, with the ever-changing technological environment, the boundary between identifiable and non-identifiable data is getting blurred. Ohm [115] remarks that—*"The list of potential PII will never stop growing until it includes everything."* This has led some researchers to question the usefulness of the very concepts of personal information and PII.

In order to better understand the concepts at stake, it is necessary to clarify the differences between identifiable and non-identifiable data: for a person to be identifiable, is it necessary to be able to determine his civil identity or home address (as suggested by Dammann and Jay above) or is it sufficient to be able to single him out, that is to say to distinguish him from all other individuals in a given group? Should the possibility to infer information about a group of people (e.g., through group profiling), without necessarily identifying any of them, be taken into consideration or not? Is it possible to truly anonymize[5] data originating from individuals, that is to say to ensure that it will be impossible to re-establish any link with the individuals in the future? How should uncertainty be taken into account (for example if links could be established with a probability of 70%)? Researchers argue that the fast evolving technological landscape, the vast amount of data available today, the various techniques to link different sources of information, all make it very difficult to draw a clear line between identifiable and non-identifiable information. What is de-identified or non-identifiable today could be re-identified or identifiable tomorrow.

For example, re-identification may result from successfully isolating *"data fingerprints,"* i.e., combinations of values of data unique to an individual and linking them to additional information, often referred to as auxiliary information [115] or background information[6] [165]. The key issue is that human beings are unique in many ways [65, 99, 100]: visited locations, watched movies,

---

[4]This does not imply that it is an absolute right though, as it may sometimes conflict with other fundamental rights such as freedom of expression, personal safety and security. Depending on the circumstances, precedence can be given to one right or another.

[5]See the work of Domingo-Ferrer et al. [42] for a survey on various privacy models for anonymization such as k-anonymity, l-diversity and t-closeness and the alternative paradigm of differential privacy.

[6]Background information is discussed in Chapter 6.

browsing history, demographic information, technical configurations, driving behavior, just to take a few examples. In addition, the type and the amount of the auxiliary information cannot be predicted due to the growing volume of information available from various sources such as social media, blogs, mobile phones, sensors, connection metadata, consumer databases, etc.

Researchers such as Ohm [115], Yakowitz [167] and Wu [165] provide different perspectives on this debate. Ohm [115] points out that weak "anonymization" (or alleged anonymization) solutions[7] are more widespread than one might think, because anonymization is a difficult topic, even for experts. This, together with the fact that the power of the risk sources is only likely to grow, at least in terms of computation power and auxiliary information, leads him to conclude that we can expect more and more cases of re-identification, raising doubts about the adequacy of the anonymization approach. Ohm concludes that privacy laws must no longer rely on the concept of PII and we should rather shift to new paradigms for information privacy regulation.

Schwartz and Solove [134] share Ohm's criticism about the notion of PII. They also believe that the distinction between PII and non-PII is blurring very quickly. However, instead of completely abandoning the concept, they propose a reconceptualization of PII, giving rise to what they call PII 2.0. They argue that one cannot completely do away with the concept of PII as it sets the boundaries of privacy statutes and regulations. According to PII 2.0, when information bears a significant risk of identification it should be treated as identifiable information, whereas if there is no risk of identification then it is referred to as non-identifiable information. Any information between these two extremes relates to situations in which identification is possible even if unlikely, which leads to a continuous rather than a binary approach to PII.

On the technical front, the Opinion 05/2014 of the Working Party 29 on anonymization techniques [13] proposes a structured approach to assess the effectiveness and limits of anonymization techniques. The Working Party 29 puts forward three criteria to assess the robustness of an anonymization technique:

1. Singling out: *"is it still possible to single out an individual"*?

2. Linking: *"is it still possible to link records relating to an individual"*?

3. Inference: *"can information be inferred concerning an individual"*?

The Working Party 29 stresses that pseudonymization is not an anonymization method but a useful security measure that can be used to reduce the linkability of a dataset with the identity of the subject. It also emphasizes that *"anonymization should not be regarded as a one-off exercise and the attending risks should be reassessed regularly by data controllers."* Even though it has also triggered some debate [46] and further clarifications are still needed, no doubt that this opinion will be a valuable tool for data protection authorities in the future.

---

[7] For example, a common practice among organizations is to release data after removing all explicit identifiers such as names, addresses and telephone numbers, assuming that the resulting data is anonymous [142]. However, in many cases the remaining data can still be used to re-identify individuals by linking it with other data or by finding unique individuals' characteristics in the data. For example, Sweeney [142] argues that a combination of the 5-digit ZIP code, the gender and the date of birth can uniquely identify about 87% of the persons in the United States.

In contrast with the negative views toward anonymization and PII in general, Yakowitz [167] argues that, when done correctly, anonymization may still be used to achieve both privacy and utility. She criticizes Ohm [115] for over-emphasizing the risks of re-identification when there are hardly any real instances of such harm scenarios. According to her, re-identification is not easy and risk sources often lack suitable incentives to engage into such activities. Along the same line, Cavoukian and Castro [24] argue that the risk of re-identification has been greatly exaggerated in previous studies,[8] but their position is criticized by Narayanan and Felten [101].

In an attempt to bridge the gap between advocates and detractors of anonymization, Wu [165] puts forward the concept of "privacy threat" as a key tool to better understand the issues at stake and find the appropriate balance between privacy and utility. Wu makes the observation that most disagreements between researchers stem from different assumptions about the risk model, including the objective of the protection (e.g., identification, sensitive attribute disclosure, or linking), the sources of risk (e.g., outsiders only, or also insiders), their background knowledge and the potential harms (only concrete harms or also emotional or psychological harms). Privacy risk analysis, as presented in this book, should provide a methodological framework to support this kind of approach.

To sum up this discussion on anonymization, there is a growing view that the frontier between anonymous data and personal data is increasingly blurred and, for this reason, it is better to rely on assessments of actual privacy risks rather than restricted definitions and fixed obligations [120, 128]. In line with this, we choose to take a definition of personal data that is as broad as possible in this book,[9] considering that the goal of the PRA is precisely to shed light on actual risks in order to prioritize actions and choose appropriate protections. The ultimate goal should be that individuals are protected against any misuse of data that could have an impact on their life.

4.3   CATEGORIES OF DATA

As discussed in Section 2.6, it is useful to rely on existing categorizations or typologies of components, in particular personal data, to minimize the risks of omission during the analysis. Table 4.1 presents a list of categories of personal data that should be considered in a privacy analysis. This list, which is based on previous cases of privacy breaches and the literature in this area, is obviously not claimed to be exhaustive. In addition, categories are generally not exclusive. As an illustration, a photograph may reveal a person's physical attributes, location, friends, and sometimes also his financial status.

In addition to their utility as checklists, categories provide information about the sensitivity of the data, which can be useful to assess the nature and the severity of potential privacy harms. The sensitivity of certain categories of data has been extensively discussed in the literature and it has

---

[8]Mostly because they relied, according to Cavoukian and Castro, on unrealistic assumptions about the background knowledge available to those who would like to re-identify data (which in turn has been challenged by Narayanan and Felten [101]).
[9]See Section 2.1.

Table 4.1: Categories of personal data

Category of Personal Data	Examples
Identification data	Name, social security number, biometric data
Contact data	Telephone number, e-mail address, home or office address
Technical data	IP address, event logs
Economic and financial data	Credit card number, bank account details, income, tax situation
Health data	Diseases, diagnostic reports, hospital, practitioner, prescriptions
Genetic data	Genetic profiles
Behavorial data	Profiles based on shopping habits and related preferences
Location data	Travel itinerary, GPS data, GSM data, ZIP code, address
Professional data	Educational qualifications, professional training, employer, profession
Data conveying information about personal life	Sex life, living habits
Data conveying information about origin	Race, ethnicity, birth location
Data conveying information about personal beliefs	Religious or philosophical beliefs, political inclinations, trade-union membership
Legal data	Criminal convictions, offenses

been enshrined into law and integrated within official recommendations. For example, according to the U.S. Department of Homeland Security [153], some PII such as social security numbers and biometric identifiers are sensitive by themselves, whereas others, such as account passwords and medical data, are sensitive when used in conjunction with the identity of an individual.

The EU Directive [47] (Article 8) does not use the term "sensitive information" but stipulates that: *"Member States shall prohibit the processing of personal data revealing racial or ethnic origin, political opinions, religious or philosophical beliefs, trade-union membership, and the processing of data concerning health or sex life."*[10]

---

[10]Some exceptions are that these special categories of data can be processed under the circumstances where the data subject has given his consent, the processing is necessary to protect vital interests of the subject, in cases of criminal convictions or for substantial public interest.

The GDPR [48], in its Recital 51, states that *"Personal data which are, by their nature, particularly sensitive in relation to fundamental rights and freedoms merit specific protection . . ."* Its Article 9 defines the categories of data to be considered sensitive[11] and this definition appears to be broader than that of the EU Directive.

In the U.S., certain regulations provide increased protection to categories of data that may not correspond exactly to "sensitive data" in the EU [135]. Generally speaking, the categories of information that have been treated as sensitive and worthy of special protection by laws in the U.S. and in Europe include: health information,[12] genetic information,[13] information on sexual behavior,[14] financial information,[15] personal safety information,[16] criminal records, education information,[17] information about children,[18] political opinions[19] and video watching information[20] [116].

Despite the importance of the notion of sensitive information, very few studies have been conducted to try to define precisely what makes certain types of data sensitive. Serwin's work [136] is one of the rare attempts to identify a set of determining factors in deciding the sensitivity of a category of data. These factors include: the nature of the information, in particular how much it reveals about a person, the level of impact caused by the disclosure of the information, the social utility of sharing the information, whether it can be used to obtain or create other information, the communication medium and the steps undertaken to protect the confidentiality of the information. Another set of factors has been proposed by Ohm [116] to determine whether a category of information should be considered sensitive: (1) the possibility of harms,[21] (2) the probability of harms,[22] (3) the presence of a confidential relationship[23] and (4) the reflection of a majoritarian harm.[24] Taken individually, these criteria are not surprising, but they had not been explicitly stated and analyzed before. They show that, in fact, the true sensitivity of a piece of data

---

[11]These categories include: racial or ethnic origin, political opinions, religious or philosophical beliefs, trade-union membership, and the processing of genetic data, biometric data for the purpose of uniquely identifying a natural person, data concerning health or data concerning a natural person's sex life or sexual orientation.

[12]Protected by Health Information Portability and Accountability Act (HIPAA), U.S.

[13]Protected by the Genetic Information Nondiscrimination Act (GINA), U.S.

[14]Protected by the EU Data Protection Directive.

[15]Protected by Gramm-Leach-Bliley Act (GLBA), U.S.

[16]Protected by Driver's Privacy Protection Act, U.S.

[17]Protected by Federal Educational Rights and Privacy Act (FERPA), U.S.

[18]Protected by Children's Online Privacy Protection Act (COPPA), U.S.

[19]Protected by the EU Data Protection Directive.

[20]Protected by Video Privacy Protection Act (VPPA), U.S.

[21]The first factor to decide whether information may be sensitive is its connection with harms. Information may be deemed sensitive if it can be used by adversaries to cause harm to data subjects or related people [116].

[22]Information is classified as sensitive if the probability of the harm is sufficiently high [116].

[23]Many privacy regulations protect information that may cause harm when held by particular parties who owe a duty of confidentiality to the data subjects due to a special relationship. For example, HIPAA protects the doctor-patient relationship.

[24]Categories of information whose disclosure might harm a large number of people are generally considered sensitive. When the revelation of a piece of information may cause harms recognized by the ruling majority, then the information is also considered sensitive. In contrast, information that causes harm to a very small number of people (and is not recognized by the ruling majority) is not considered sensitive. Therefore, according to this definition, sensitive information does not cover all types of privacy harms.

can be determined only through an in-depth privacy risk analysis, taking into account the severity and likelihood of privacy harms resulting from the misuse of the data [116].

4.4 PERSONAL DATA ATTRIBUTES

In order to conduct a privacy risk analysis, it is necessary not only to know the categories of personal data at stake, but also to characterize them precisely. The literature on privacy discusses the various aspects of data and their relationship to privacy: identifiability [62, 134], sensitivity [33, 116, 136], visibility [14], granularity [14, 52], retention period [14], the purpose of data collection [14], data origin and control [131], intervenability [171], etc. In this section, we suggest a set of data attributes that encompasses all the important aspects of data discussed in the literature and can be used as a basis for performing a privacy risk analysis.

Some of these attributes may have slightly different meanings or may be assigned different values in each phase of the data lifecycle. We consider three main phases here: (1) collection, (2) processing and (3) dissemination.[25] Data attributes related to the collection of data describe the data as it enters the system while those corresponding to the processing phase describe the data inside the system and the dissemination phase concerns the data output from the system. Data attributes can be broadly classified into four types:

1. Data attributes related to the nature of the data.

2. Data attributes related to the format of the data.

3. Data attributes related to the context of data collection, processing and dissemination.

4. Data attributes related to the control exercised by different stakeholders on the data.

Each attribute can be assigned values in one of the following ways:

1. *Qualitatively*, for example using a fixed scale such as {low, medium, high}, or

2. *Quantitatively*, either from a fixed set of values (such as {1,2,3}) or from an unbounded set of values (natural numbers, real numbers, etc.).

In the next sections we discuss the above types of data attributes. Some of these attributes are interrelated. Nevertheless it is advisable in a privacy risk analysis to consider all of them to minimize possible oversights that could lead to erroneous risk analysis results.

4.4.1 ATTRIBUTES RELATED TO THE NATURE OF THE DATA

Some data attributes are related to the intrinsic nature of the data:

---

[25]Although we have adopted the definition of the EU Directive for the notion of "data processing," which includes dissemination and collection, we treat these steps in different phases here because they may lead to different types of threats.

1. *Sensitivity.* As discussed in Section 4.3, certain categories of data are considered *sensitive* and are granted enhanced protection by law. Beyond legal requirements, sensitivity can be used as a flag in a risk analysis, warning the analyst that this category of data deserves particular attention.

2. *Uniqueness.* Uniqueness is the fact that a particular piece of data is sufficient to uniquely identify a person. It is akin to the identifiability criterion used in the CNIL guidelines [32, 33]. For example, a social security number uniquely identifies a person. In contrast, a name may not be uniquely identifying and may require the help of other data such as city or physical attributes to uniquely identify an individual.

   Uniqueness can be characterized by a boolean value (unique or not), a discrete value [32, 33] or by a statistical value. Uniqueness may depend on other data attributes such as precision and volume.[26]

   It should be noted that uniqueness is defined as an attribute of a single piece of data here: the risk that a dataset leads to re-identification (even if none of the data taken individually meets the uniqueness criterion) is to be established by the risk analysis itself.

4.4.2   ATTRIBUTES RELATED TO THE FORMAT OF THE DATA

The format of the data can also have an impact on privacy risks. We distinguish the following format attributes (which are not necessarily useful or meaningful for all categories of data):

1. *Representation.* Most data categories can be represented in different ways, for example as pieces of *text*, *numbers* or *pictures* (e.g., an X-ray plates, holiday pictures). In some cases, a picture may reveal more information than a piece of text. For example, the picture of a person may capture, in addition to his physical appearance, details about his environment, home, car or friends.

2. *Form.* The form attribute informs on potential transformations undergone by the data (e.g., encryption, perturbation). The form of a piece of data may change as it is processed by the system. For example, data may be collected in raw format and then be encrypted during processing. It may also be encrypted before dissemination. Encryption, noise and perturbation limit the accessibility or accuracy of the data. So the form in which data is available has significant implications in terms of privacy.

3. *Precision.* Most categories of data can be defined at different levels of precision or granularity. For example, the age of an individual may be defined by a precise birth date, a number of years or a range (such as teenager, or 13–18). Similarly, a location can be defined in different ways such as exact map coordinates, a postal code or the range of a cellular antenna. Fine-grained data lead to higher privacy risks by revealing specific information about individuals.

---

[26]The precision and volume attributes are defined in Section 4.4.2.

Like the form, the precision can change during the data lifecycle. For example, fine grained data can be generalized into coarse grained data to protect privacy.

4. *Volume.* The volume attribute provides information about the number of data items involved, for example how frequently (e.g., daily, weekly, monthly) data is collected by the system. As an illustration, hourly location updates on a social network can reveal the workplace of a user, even though he does not explicitly refer to it, whereas monthly updates may not be sufficient to infer this type of information. Similarly, smart electricity meters can send energy consumption data at different frequencies (every fifteen minutes, hourly, daily, etc.), with very different impacts on privacy [98].

4.4.3   ATTRIBUTES RELATED TO THE CONTEXT

It is widely agreed that the context in which the data processing takes place is an important factor to analyze privacy breaches [104]. The following attributes can be used to provide contextual information about the data:

1. *Origin.* Data may be collected in a wide variety of ways which can lead to different types of harms. First, data may originate either from the data subject or from a third party. We call data provided by a third party (such as a friend's post about the data subject on a social networking site) *third party data.* Such data may be erroneous, defamatory or embarrassing and may lead to different types of privacy harms. Another type of origin is the inference of new information from the data that is already available. We call this *derived data.* For example, in some cases, it may be possible to derive the approximate age of the data subject, his origin or even his sexual orientation from the list of his links in a social network. Both accurate and inaccurate predictions may lead to different types of harms for the subject.

   In general, data subjects need to provide certain pieces of information (for example, name, age and e-mail address for social networks) as a requirement to get access to a service or to be a part of a group. We call this *required disclosure.* Some service providers take advantage of the situation and collect more data than necessary, violating the principle of data minimization, by making them mandatory to get access to their services.

   Once he gets access to a service or is a part of a community, the user may disclose further information deliberately, for example when using a search engine or a social network. We refer to this as *deliberate disclosure.* Users may often reveal on their own initiative more information than they should, due to misjudgment of the potential risks [63].

   Data may also be collected implicitly from a data subject. This is the case, for instance, with IP addresses and various pieces of technical information collected during browsing (OS configuration, browser type, operating system fonts, etc.). We call this *implicit collection.* Most users are not aware of all implicit data collections occurring in the digital world and hence cannot comprehend their implications in terms of privacy.

2. *Purpose.* The purpose defines the reason why the data is collected, processed or disseminated. The definition of a specific purpose (and use of the data consistently with this declaration) is an obligation in the EU according to the EU Directive [47]. If the data controller does not comply with the obligations related to the purpose, there is a privacy risk for the subject because his expectations about the processing are not met and his data may be used in an unfair manner.

3. *Retention.* The amount of time during which a piece of data is retained in a system should be proportionate to the purpose of its collection. The value of this attribute may vary depending on the form of the data. For example, a system can ensure that raw data is deleted as soon as it is anonymized during the processing phase, while anonymized data may be stored for a longer period of time.

4.4.4   ATTRIBUTES RELATED TO CONTROL

Another aspect which can have an impact on privacy risks is the type of control or access that the subject (and other parties) may have on the data. Two dimensions of control can be distinguished: *visibility* and *intervenability*.

1. *Visibility.* Visibility refers to the number and types of stakeholders having access to the data. Other things being equal, data with less visibility present fewer privacy risks. For example, a piece of data posted by the user of a social network may be visible only to him and the service provider, also to his friends, or also to friends of friends, or to all the users of the network, which is the most risky scenario. Visibility may evolve through the data lifecycle and may depend on the form of the data (e.g., encrypted or not).

2. *Intervenability.* The notion of intervenability [171] characterizes the possibility for the data subject or the data controller to intervene when required. This includes the fact that a data subject can get access to his data, can know who has access to it, delete it, update, modify or rectify it, get it back (portability) or raise an alarm in case of harm. Similarly, a data controller should be able to intervene if the processing leads to privacy harms, ideally by putting an end to the cause of the harm. Intervenability is a form of control over personal data and it may help reduce the effects of privacy harms.

4.5   ILLUSTRATION: THE BEMS SYSTEM

We proceed with the BEMS System introduced in Section 3.2 to illustrate personal data components and attributes. The billing and energy management sub-systems of the BEMS System involve the following categories of personal data:

1. Identification and contact data: name, home address, e-mail address, phone number, date of birth, meter identifier, user portal account number.

2. Information about energy consumption.

3. Information related to billing: bill, energy management suggestions, payment status, bank account number.

As an illustration, we describe some relevant data attributes for energy consumption data. All attributes are shown in Table 4.2, and Table 4.3 focuses on the *visibility* attribute.

1. Attributes related to the nature of the data:

    (a) *Sensitivity.* Electricity consumption data is not considered sensitive with respect to the law.[27]

    (b) *Uniqueness.* Electricity consumption data can be unique when they are sufficiently precise and frequent (which is the case with the assumptions adopted here).

2. Attributes related to the format of the data:

    (a) *Representation.* Numeric.

    (b) *Form.* Not encrypted or signed during transmission from home appliance to the smart meter, encrypted and signed during transmission in the rest of the system. Encrypted when stored. Not encrypted during processing. Any system or application or actor must authenticate itself before getting access to this data.

    (c) *Precision.* Precise kilowatt-hour measure per user.

    (d) *Volume.* Collected every 15 minutes.[28]

3. Attributes related to the context:

    (a) *Origin.* Required data, implicitly collected from consumers.

    (b) *Purpose.* To produce bills and energy management suggestions.

    (c) *Retention.* Five years.

4. Related to control:

    (a) *Visibility.* Visible to the MDMS and the PMS administrators.

    (b) *Intervenability.* None for the consumer.

---

[27]It does not belong to the list of data considered sensitive in the EU Directive or GDPR and we do not know of any regulation granting a specific status to electricity consumption data, even though this type of data can be used to infer sensitive information such as religious belief.

[28]This is an assumption about the BEMS System. Different frequencies are adopted by different countries.

Table 4.2: BEMS data attribute values (*Continues.*)

Data Attribute	Data Categories										
	Name	Address	E-mail, Phone #	DoB	Meter ID	User Portal Account #	Bill	Payment Status	Bank Account #	Energy Mgmt.	Energy Consumption
Sensitivity	Not sensitive	Not sensitive	Not sensitive	Not sensitive	Not sensitive	Not sensitive	Not sensitive	Not sensitive	Not sensitive	Not sensitive	Not sensitive
Uniqueness	May be unique	May be unique	Unique	May be unique	Unique	Unique	Not unique	Not unique	Unique	May be unique	May be unique
Representation	Alphabetic	Alpha-numeric	Numeric	Numeric	Numeric	Numeric	Alpha-numeric	Alpha-numeric	Alpha-numeric	Alpha-numeric	Numeric
Form					Unencrypted during processing, encrypted otherwise						
Precision	Full name per user	Full address per user	Per user	DD/MM/YYYY, per user	Per user	Per user	Break-up based on different tariff, per user	Per user	Per user	Per time period (based on tariff variation), per user	Kilowatt-hour per user
Volume	One	One	One	One	One	One	Per billing cycle	Per billing cycle	One	Per billing cycle	Every 15 minutes
Origin	Required	Required	Required	Required	Derived	Derived	Derived	Derived	Required	Derived	Required/implicit

Table 4.2: (Continued.) BEMS data attribute values

Data Attribute	Data Categories										
	Name	Address	E-mail, Phone #	DoB	Meter ID	User Portal Account #	Bill	Payment Status	Bank Account #	Energy Mgmt.	Energy Consumption
Purpose[29]	Identifying, contacting consumers (CIS)				Maps to consumer identification and meter assigned to him (UI, CIS, BA, EMA, PA)	Identifies consumer for online access to his account (UI, URS, CIS)	To inform consumer about payment due, for energy management, computation of payment status (BA, CIS, PA)	To track due payments w.r.t bills (CIS, PA)	For billing (CIS, PA)	To inform user about better home energy management practices (EMA)	For billing, energy management (BA, EMA)
Retention	Until user stops using the service or 5 years (for dispute resolution) whichever is larger.						5 years	5 years	Until user stops using service	5 years	5 years
Visibility	Admin., operator of CIS, consumer, service technician			Admin., operator of CIS, consumer	Admin., operator of MDMS, UI, CIS, PMS, service technician, consumer	Admin., operator of UI, URS, CIS, consumer	Admin. of CIS, PMS, consumer	Admin. of CIS, PMS, consumer	Admin. of CIS, PMS, consumer	Admin. of CIS, PMS, consumer	Admin. of PMS, MDMS
Intervenability	Correction	Correction / update	Correction / update	Correction	None	None	Challenge	Challenge	Update	Opt out	None

[29] Here, for each type of data we mention the broad purpose of usage and the applications/systems which use it.

Table 4.3: BEMS visibility attribute

Actor	Data Categories										
	Name	Address	E-mail, Phone #	DoB	Meter ID	User Portal Account #	Bill	Payment Status	Bank Account #	Energy Mgmt.	Energy Consumption
Consumer (Data subject)	✓	✓	✓	✓	✓	✓	✓	✓	✓	✓	✗
MDMS administrator	✗	✗	✗	✗	✓	✗	✗	✗	✗	✗	✓
MDMS operators	✗	✗	✗	✗	✓	✗	✗	✗	✗	✗	✗
UI administrator	✗	✗	✗	✗	✓	✓	✗	✗	✗	✗	✗
UI operators	✗	✗	✗	✗	✓	✓	✗	✗	✗	✗	✗
CIS administrator	✓	✓	✓	✓	✓	✓	✓	✓	✓	✓	✗
CIS operators	✓	✓	✓	✓	✓	✓	✗	✗	✗	✗	✗
URS administrator	✗	✗	✗	✗	✗	✓	✗	✗	✗	✗	✗
URS operators	✗	✗	✗	✗	✗	✓	✗	✗	✗	✗	✗
PDS administrator	✗	✗	✗	✗	✗	✗	✗	✗	✗	✗	✗
PDS operators	✗	✗	✗	✗	✗	✗	✗	✗	✗	✗	✗
PMS administrator	✗	✗	✗	✗	✓	✗	✓	✓	✓	✓	✓
PMS operators	✗	✗	✗	✗	✓	✗	✗	✗	✗	✗	✗
Service technicians	✓	✓	✓	✗	✓	✗	✗	✗	✗	✗	✗
Other employees under service provider	✗	✗	✗	✗	✗	✗	✗	✗	✗	✗	✗
Third-parties	✗	✗	✗	✗	✗	✗	✗	✗	✗	✗	✗

CHAPTER 5

Stakeholders

The stakeholders are the entities that are concerned, in one way or another, by the processing of the personal data. They include the individuals to whom the data relates (or who can be affected by the processing of the data) and the entities taking part in the processing of the data or having (legally or illegally) access to it. Identifying all stakeholders is a key step in a privacy risk analysis because it helps the analyst determine the persons to be protected and the entities that can act on the data and should be responsible for their protection. It can also provide useful information to identify the potential risk sources (which are discussed in the next chapter).

We start with a sketch of the different types of stakeholders found in the literature (Section 5.1) before suggesting a minimal set of stakeholder categories and stakeholder attributes that should be considered in a privacy risk analysis (Section 5.2 and Section 5.3). Finally, we describe the stakeholders and their attributes for our running example, the BEMS System (Section 5.4).

5.1 THE NATURE OF THE STAKEHOLDERS

Table C.1 in Appendix C displays the definitions of various stakeholders as provided by regulations and standards in the EU and the U.S. For example, the CNIL guidelines [32] use the definitions of data subject and data controller from the French Data Protection Act [50]. As noted in Chapter 2, the definitions of the stakeholders do not generally require that they comply with the law. For example, a data controller may collect excessive amounts of data or not comply with the purpose limitation principle.

The EU Directive [47] describes four types of stakeholders: data controllers, data processors, third parties and data subjects, whereas the French Data Protection Act [50] only defines data subjects and data controllers. The ISO/IEC 29100:2011 document [72] refers to the data subject as the "PII principal." It also defines the notions of "PII controller" and "PII processor." Table C.1 shows that, in the same way as for the definition of personal data, U.S. laws such as HIPAA and COPPA define the stakeholders for specific sectors (healthcare and child protection respectively).

Solove [140] refers to two types of stakeholders: "data subjects" and "data holders." While other definitions of data subjects characterize them as the persons to whom the data relates, Solove [140] takes a more general view and includes any individual whose life can be "most directly" affected by the use of the data. Data holders can collect, process, store, manipulate, search and use data. These activities are together referred to as information processing by Solove [140], where the meaning of the term "processing" is consistent with the definition of the EU Directive [47]. Data holders can also release the information or transfer it to other stakeholders.

In the context of database management systems, Barker et al. [14] define the notions of "provider," "collector" and "third parties." A provider is an *individual or organization providing data that is to be stored or used.*" The provider may or may not be the data subject.[1] Similarly, they define a collector as an *individual or organization that initially collects, uses, or stores data received from the provider.*" A third party is *any individual or organization that acquires the provided data from the collector.*" Even though their definition of collector is close to the notion of "data controller" in Europe, they do not refer to the fact that collectors can decide the purpose and the means of data processing.

In a privacy risk analysis, the objective is generally the protection of the privacy of data subjects. In the context of database privacy, Domingo-Ferrer [41] distinguishes three types of stakeholders: the respondent, the owner of the database and the user of the database. The respondents are the individuals whose data is stored in the database. The user is the actor who queries the database. Following the European terminology, when the user is an individual, he is a particular type of subject whose personal data are the queries themselves. The protection of the owner is the protection of the dataset from unauthorized access, which can be seen as a traditional security (confidentiality) property.

The Working Party 29 [8] sheds some light on the definitions of controller and processor in the EU Directive [47].[2] Compared to other definitions of data controller in [50] and [72], the EU Directive introduces the notion of joined control when it states that the data controller can determine the purposes and the means of processing personal data *either alone or jointly with others.*" It broadens the meaning of the term "controller," allowing it to encompass multiple stakeholders taking part in the processing. The EU Directive also makes the controller responsible for setting the conditions enabling lawful data processing and for enabling data subjects to exercise their rights in practice.

The EU Directive [47] stipulates that the purpose of the data processing must be decided by the controller, whereas it can delegate decisions regarding the means of the processing. According to the interpretation of the Working Party 29 [8], the controller only needs to decide the *effective means* of the processing. These are *substantial questions* that are *essential to the core of the processing,*" such as which data to process, for how long, who should have access to the data and when it should be deleted. They do not encompass technical or organizational questions. Such questions are delegated to the processors. The processor has a certain leeway in deciding the means of processing such as the hardware or the software to use. The processors may also delegate parts of the processing to sub-contractors. However, at all levels, processors and sub-processors must abide by the instructions of the data controller. The key issue is to clearly allocate responsibilities and obligations arising from the data processing activities.

---

[1]In the European terminology, the data subject is the person to whom the data relates.
[2]Interested readers can find these definitions in Appendix C.

Schwartz [133] and Hon et al. [69] argue that there remains considerable ambiguity on whether a cloud service provider is a controller or a processor when data is processed in the cloud and the decision should depend on the actual context. Hon et al. [69] provide a series of compelling arguments to show that: (1) cloud service providers providing equipment and software to their customers to process personal data are not processors themselves and (2) automatic caching of data due to the customer's use of the cloud provider's software does not make the hardware or the software provider a processor. However, if the data is saved in the permanent storage of the cloud service provider, then the provider is likely to be a processor. Whether such data has to be considered as personal data greatly depends on whether it is encrypted or anonymized. For example, if the cloud service provider provides storage for encrypted data for which it does not have access to the decryption key, then it should not be considered as a data controller for this data. However, the authors point out that the status of a cloud provider should not be dependent on the strength of the encryption or the anonymization techniques chosen by its customers as these choices, in most cases, are beyond its knowledge and control.

Hon et al. [69] also argue that, in the absence of unauthorized behaviors[3] and given that sufficient measures have been adopted by the cloud service provider to prevent unauthorized accesses, it is unreasonable to burden the cloud service provider with the liabilities of a controller or a processor. In the context of cloud computing that may involve a complex chain of providers and sub-providers, it is often difficult to determine which parties decide upon the "means" of processing. Therefore, according to Hon et al. [69], the simple, binary approach of assigning either the role of controller or the role of processor to providers is not satisfactory. They advocate the approach of imposing the primary liability on one party, assigning different degrees of responsibility and liability to other stakeholders in proportion to the role that each of them plays in the processing chain. The goal of the rule would be to encourage the parties to take appropriate protection measures and to contractually allocate risks and responsibilities.

5.2   STAKEHOLDER CATEGORIES

Based on the above discussion, we suggest the consideration of the following four categories of stakeholders in a privacy risk analysis:

1. Data subjects, who are the identified or identifiable natural persons whom the personal data relate to (see Definition 2.3).

2. Data controllers, which are entities (individuals or organizations) that, alone or jointly with others, determine the purpose, conditions and means of processing of personal data (see Definition 2.4).

3. Data processors, which are entities (individuals or organizations) that process personal data on behalf of a data controller (see Definition 2.5).

---

[3]Such as providing access to data to third parties without any authorization from the customer or using the data for its own purposes.

4. Third parties, which are entities (individuals or organizations) other than data subjects, controllers, processors and the persons who, under the direct authority of a controller or a processor, are authorized to process the data (see Definition 2.6).

5.3   STAKEHOLDER ATTRIBUTES

In addition to the nature of the stakeholders, a privacy risk analysis should take into account the possible connections between them, in particular their relationships and communications.

1. *Relationships.* The relationships between the stakeholders can have an impact on privacy risks. These relationships (e.g., employer-employee, provider-customer, friendship) may induce power relations. Unbalanced relationships may put the weaker party in a difficult position when he is the victim of illegal or unfair practices. For example, when organizations with large user databases decide to change their privacy policy or their practices, then their users may suffer harms without being able to do much to remedy the situation. Any hierarchical relationship may lead to similar problems. Trust relationships should also be taken into account. For example, an individual who has been the customer of a bank for many years may tend to trust the bank based on his positive experience. However, he may not trust another bank in which he has recently opened an account. A betrayal from a trusted stakeholder is likely to be more harmful to the victim as he may be caught off-guard.

2. *Communications.* The potential communications between the stakeholders is also a useful piece of information in a privacy risk analysis. Data originates from the data subject or from another stakeholder and flows to the data controller. The flow may end at the controller, unless it delegates the processing to data processors or sends the data to third parties. Data processors may further give access to the data to sub-processors. The data flow view should make it possible to identify all the stakeholders that can have access to the data.

   The communications attribute discussed here should not be confused with the data flow diagram introduced in Section 3.1,[4] which defines the flows of data within the system rather than between stakeholders.

5.4   ILLUSTRATION: THE BEMS SYSTEM

We assume three stakeholders for the analysis of the BEMS System: the consumer[5] (data subject), the utility provider (data controller), and the bank (third party). The data controller uses the services of the bank for the payments of the bills. The stakeholder attributes are defined as follows:

1. *Relationships.* Consumers do not have any choice in the amount of data that is collected. Moreover, the energy management services come bundled with billing, i.e., consumers receive bills with all energy saving related information, unless they choose to opt out of the

---

[4]Even though they may overlap when the system under consideration encompasses several stakeholders.
[5]Also referred to as user or customer in the sequel.

latter. Even when they opt out of the energy management services, the data controller still collects their data at the same level of precision and volume. Therefore, the consumers do not have much incentive to opt out. The utility provider also installs the smart meter and the utility gateway at the consumer premises. Therefore, the consumer may face hassles if he decides to change his utility provider to one that does not support smart meters. Based on these observations, we can conclude that consumers are in a weak position in relation to the utility provider.

2. *Communications.*

- The consumer's identification and contact information flow from the data subject to the data controller during user registration.
- Energy consumption data flow from home appliances to the data controller.
- Payment data flow from the banks to the data controller.

CHAPTER 6

Risk Sources

One of the first questions to be addressed in any type of risk analysis is: what are the potential sources of risk? The sources of risk are the entities whose actions can lead to a privacy breach. Theses entities are often referred to as "adversaries" or "attackers" in the security literature but we prefer to use the term "risk source" here as it is less security-laden and it is not limited to malicious third parties. For example, the data controller itself represents a source of risk for the data subject. The CNIL guidelines [32, 33] also use the expression "risk sources" and define them as insiders (such as employees of the data controller) or outsiders (such as competitors or hackers) that can cause risk, accidentally or deliberately. Risk sources having close relationships with data subjects should also be considered because they have significantly more background information than the general public [165]. A privacy risk analysis should consider in a systematic way all risk sources, including risk sources related to the data controller (the data controller itself, its processors, sub-contractors, customers, etc.), risk sources related to data subjects (relatives, friends, collegues, etc.), risk sources related to the states (intelligence agencies, police enforcement bodies, etc.) and generic risk sources (data brokers, hackers, etc.).

The two most important characteristics of risk sources in the context of a privacy risk analysis are their motivation to undertake privacy invasive actions and their capacity to carry them out. Some researchers have studied the motivation factor in a theoretical way, in particular with respect to re-identification. For example, Wan et al. [157] have defined a game theoretic framework based on the assumption that a risk source is likely to perform a re-identification only when the potential gains outweigh the costs. Their model takes into account the cost to perform a re-identification and the probability of success. However, no general studies have been carried out to date on risk sources for privacy and their relevant attributes.

We first present a list of risk source attributes that must be taken into account in a privacy risk analysis (Section 6.1) before showing their application to the BEMS System (Section 6.2).

6.1 RISK SOURCE ATTRIBUTES

For the purpose of a privacy risk analysis, at least three classes of risk source attributes should be taken into account: (1) attributes defining their nature, (2) attributes characterizing their motivation and (3) attributes characterizing their capacities. The attributes of the first class are useful to define the attributes of the two other classes.

6.1.1 NATURE OF THE RISK SOURCES

The two most important attributes related to the nature of a risk source are its type and its relationships with other stakeholders.

1. *Type.* Risk sources may be of various types: they may be individuals, groups of individuals, organizations or even states. An individual risk source is likely to be weaker in terms of resources than an organization or a state. In addition, an organization may have other powers that may strengthen its position, such as political power or the power to influence data subjects or other stakeholders. In contrast with [33], we consider that a malicious code such as a virus or a worm has been created and disseminated by human beings and can therefore be considered as a tool used by the true (human) risk source rather than a risk source itself.

2. *Relationships.* Another key piece of information about a risk source is its potential relationships with other stakeholders. As discussed above, a risk source can have close relationships with the data subject or the data controller, which can yield significant advantages to carry out a privacy breach. The terms "internal risk sources" or "insiders" are often used to refer to risk sources such as disgruntled employees who can get easier access to the information system through the data controller. Other risk sources are sometimes called "external risk sources" or "outsiders." Similarly, any third party trusted by the data subject can become a powerful risk source if he tries to take advantage of the situation.

   Another type of relationship to be considered in a risk analysis is collusion. This possibility should not be overlooked as it can significantly enhance the power of the risk sources.

6.1.2 MOTIVATION

The level of motivation of a risk source depends on two main factors: the incentives and the disincentives to engage in harmful actions.

1. *Incentives.* The incentives include all benefits that a risk source might expect from a feared event. It can been seen as the counterpart of privacy harms (adverse consequences of the feared events on data subjects) from the point of view of the risk source. Incentives can be of very different types [66–68, 97, 156]: financial gain, prestige, ego satisfaction, retaliation, political objectives, etc.

2. *Disincentives.* Disincentives include all factors that could hold the risk source back from causing a feared event. Potential disincentives are also varied: financial (potential losses), legal (risk of legal proceedings), loss of trust from customers, damage to image, etc.

   In practice, the motivation of a risk source may be very different for different feared events.

6.1.3 RESOURCES

Different types of resources can affect the capacity of a risk source to cause privacy harms:

1. *Background information.* Background information about data subjects can be useful to a risk source, for example to re-identify subjects in a dataset or to infer further information about them. Re-identification is discussed in Section 4.2.

2. *Access rights.* Some risk sources may be authorized to access certain personal data. This can typically be the case for internal risk sources (e.g., system administrators) who are trusted by the data controller and for relatives who are trusted by the data subject.

3. *Tools and skills.* Some risk sources (for example, hackers and states) may have access to powerful tools and technologies and have more skills than others to exploit privacy weaknesses.

4. *Computational power.* The amount of storage and processing capacity available to a risk source is also an important factor in the context of a privacy risk analysis. Organizations and states typically have greater computation power than individual risk sources.

The above risk source attributes have been discussed extensively in the literature. For example, Wu [165] has studied threat modeling based on the specification of the goals and capabilities of the risk sources (including background information and computational power). The CNIL guidelines [32] also refer to the identification of the risk sources and their capabilities.

6.2 ILLUSTRATION: THE BEMS SYSTEM

Three general categories of risk sources should be considered for a smart meter system:

- Individuals (e.g., disgruntled employees)

- Organizations (e.g., the utility provider itself, external organizations)

- Criminals

The most relevant risk sources for the BEMS System and their attributes are shown in Table 6.1.

Table 6.1: BEMS risk sources and attributes

Risk Source	Type	Relationships	Incentives	Disincentives	Background Information	Access Rights	Tools and Skills	Computation Power
Utility provider	Organization	Insider	Financial gain	Loss of trust, image among consumers	May have access to other information about consumers	All data	High	High
System administrator	Individual	Insider	Retaliation, financial gain, etc.	Loss of job or other penalties	Limited	Selective (see Table 4.3)	Medium	Medium
System operator	Individual	Insider	Retaliation, financial gain, etc.	Loss of job or other penalties	Limited	Selective (see Table 4.3)	Medium	Medium
Service technician	Individual	Insider	Retaliation, financial gain, etc.	Loss of job or other penalties	Limited	Name and contact information, meter ID	Medium	Low
Rogue employee (other than sys. admin. or service tech. or operator)	Individual	Insider	Retaliation, financial gain, etc.	Loss of job or other penalties	Limited	None	Low	Low
Hacker	Individual/ organization	Outsider	Financial gain, thrill, etc.	Legal penalties	Likely to have access to more information about consumers	None	High	High

CHAPTER 7

Feared Events

We use the expression "feared event" to denote the events (in the technical sense) of the processing system that should be avoided because they may lead to privacy harms. The privacy harm itself is the impact of a feared event on people (data subjects, groups, society). Different privacy harms may result from the same feared event, and different feared events may lead to the same privacy harm. For example, the unauthorized disclosure or publication of personal data is a feared event because it can be defined as a technical event. This feared event can cause privacy harms such as damaged reputation, family breakdown or even suicide. Other examples of feared events include data aggregation and data inference, which can lead to harms of varying severity such as embarrassing advertising emails or discrimination. The succession of actions leading to a feared event is often called an "attack" or a "threat" in the computer security area but we prefer to use the expression "harm scenario" here to avoid the security flavor and to stress the fact that the regular use of the system can sometimes give rise to privacy breaches.[1] The privacy literature does not always use the above terms consistently and does not reflect the clear distinction made here between them, in particular between harms and feared events.

We discuss the variations in terminology (Section 7.1) before presenting the main categories and the attributes of feared events to be considered in a privacy risk analysis (Section 7.2 and Section 7.3). Finally, we illustrate the categories and attributes of feared events with the BEMS System (Section 7.4).

7.1 VARIATIONS IN TERMINOLOGY

The main inspiration for the definition adopted in this book is the CNIL guide [32] which characterizes a feared event as a *"breach of personal data security likely to have impacts on data subjects' privacy."* Alternative wordings for "feared event" in the literature include "privacy violation" [140], "privacy problem" [140], "privacy harm" [63, 124, 140] or "threat" [26, 52]. Some authors such as Solove [140] and Reidenberg [124] do not make the distinction between feared events and harms, possibly because they analyze the issue from the legal perspective. For example, Solove [140] considers, in the same list of *"information dissemination harms,"* inter alia, breach of confidentiality, disclosure and blackmail. Breach of confidentiality (e.g., unauthorized access to personal data) and disclosure are feared events in our terminology because they can be defined as technical events (events of the processing system). In contrast, blackmail is a privacy harm according to our defi-

---

[1]For the same reasons as those for which we use the wording "privacy weakness" rather than "vulnerability" and "risk source" rather than "attacker."

nitions because it is not an event of the processing system: it is the potential impact on a person of a feared event such as a breach of confidentiality. Reidenberg [124] also provides a classification of "privacy harms" based on their causes, i.e., feared events in our terminology.

Laurie et al. [81] discuss the notion of "abuse" that leads to harms in the context of health data. According to their definition, abuses include, inter alia, data theft, the fabrication or falsification of data, and the unauthorized disclosure or access to data, which are feared events in our terminology.

The CIPL report [26] states that threats lead to privacy harms, but the report does not provide a more precise definition of these terms. Examples of threats in [26] include, amongst others, excessive data collection, the use or storage of inaccurate data, data loss and unauthorized access to data, which are feared events in our terminology. Similarly, Oetzel and Spiekermann [106] state that threats prevent reaching privacy targets, where "privacy targets" are defined as privacy protection requirements stemming from EU privacy laws. In Friginal et al. [51, 52], threat sources lead to threat events that affect privacy assets. They do not differentiate between threats and feared events and focus on one specific type of threat, the disclosure of assets.

7.2 FEARED EVENT CATEGORIES

Different categories of feared events can occur at different phases of the data lifecycle, from data collection to data deletion. The main categories of feared events to be considered in a privacy risk analysis are the following:

1. Data collection

2. Data access

3. Data modification

4. Data usage

5. Data inference (including re-identification)

6. Data disclosure (including publication and dissemination)

7. Data retention

Data access is limited to reading the data, while data usage is using it for a given purpose. Data inference can be seen as a particular case of data usage but it deserves particular attention because it generates new personal information, very often without data subjects being aware of it. In general, the above events will be considered as feared events when they are excessive (e.g., excessive data collection, excessive data retention, etc.), unauthorized or unexpected by the data subject (e.g., unauthorized access, use for unauthorized purpose, unauthorized disclosure, etc.).

However, as discussed in Chapter 2, privacy harms (hence feared events) can sometimes result from the regular use of a processing system.[2]

The above categories bear similarities with Solove's taxonomy of privacy [140] which relies on four broad categories: (1) *information collection* (surveillance, interrogation), (2) *information processing* (aggregation, identification, insecurity, secondary use, exclusion), (3) *information dissemination* (breach of confidentiality, disclosure, exposure, increased accessibility, blackmail, appropriation, distortion) and (4) *invasion* (intrusion, decisional interference). The fourth category in Solove's taxonomy is of a different nature because it does not necessarily involve information. In the words of Solove, *"intrusion involves invasions or incursions into one's life. It disturbs the victim's daily activities, alters her routines, destroys her solitude, and often makes her feel uncomfortable and uneasy."* In our terminology, invasion would be considered as a privacy harm rather than a feared event.

7.3 FEARED EVENT ATTRIBUTES

In the context of a privacy risk analysis, it is useful to characterize each feared event with at least the following attributes:

1. *Scale.* The scale characterizes the number of stakeholders directly or indirectly concerned by the feared event. The first stakeholders to be considered are obviously the potential victims. For example, the disclosure of genetic data concerns the data subjects and their family. In some cases, the extent of the availability of the data (i.e., how many people may have access to the disclosed data: only one person, a couple of friends, friends of friends, anyone, etc.) should also be taken into account.

2. *Irreversibility.* The second attribute characterizes the extent to which the effect of the feared event can be cancelled out. For example, it is possible to put an end to excessive data retention[3] but the public disclosure of information on the Internet is impossible to cancel out in practice. Irreversibility is obviously an aggravating factor in the evaluation of the risks.

3. *Harm scenarios.* As discussed in Chapter 2, a harm scenario is a succession of events or actions leading to a feared event (Definition 2.10). Each feared event should therefore be associated with the set of harm scenarios that can make it happen. Methods that can be used to find such scenarios are discussed in Chapter 9.

4. *Likelihood.* As stated, for example, in Recital 90 of the GDPR,[4] one of the outputs of a privacy risk analysis is the likelihood of each type of risk. Considering that privacy harms are caused by feared events, it is necessary to assess the likelihood of all relevant feared events.

---

[2]For example, video-surveillance systems can lead to anxiety or cause changes of behavior due to the chilling effect.
[3]By deleting the data.
[4]*"In such cases, a data protection impact assessment should be carried out by the controller prior to the processing in order to assess the particular likelihood and severity of the high risk, taking into account the nature, scope, context and purposes of the processing and the sources of the risk."*

This likelihood can be evaluated based on the likelihoods of the harm scenarios leading to the feared event, which in turn depend on the capacity of the risk sources to exploit the privacy weaknesses of the information system. The evaluation of these likelihoods is discussed in Chapter 9.

7.4   ILLUSTRATION: THE BEMS SYSTEM

The most relevant feared events and associated attributes for the BEMS System are shown in Table 7.1. We do not present the likelihood attribute at this stage. Its evaluation and the precise definition of the harm scenarios are described in Chapter 9.

1. *Scale*. Depending on the actual harm scenario and the risk source, the scale of a feared event may vary. A rogue system administrator may either target one consumer and reveal his personal data or provide unauthorized access to the personal data of many consumers. For the sake of conciseness, we consider only the most likely scenarios for each feared event. For example, the data controller is more likely to collect excessive amounts of data for all its consumers rather than to target only one or a small group of consumers.

2. *Irreversibility*. We consider two factors that can have an impact on irreversibility: the extent of exposure of a consumer's personal data and the technical difficulty to reverse the consequences of a feared event. For example, if the utility provider does not provide consumers any opportunity to update incorrect information about themselves or to challenge inaccurate bills, then the feared events concerning these data will be difficult to reverse. Similarly, if the utility provider does not implement strict access control rules and all its employees can get access to consumer data or if the data is revealed to the public, then cancelling out the effect of the corresponding feared events is practically impossible. As for the scale attribute, the value assigned for irreversibility depends on the particular harm scenario and risk source. Again, we consider only the most likely scenarios and risk sources for each feared event.

We use the following values for the scale attribute:

- *Low*: the feared event affects only a single or very few individuals.

- *Medium*: the feared event affects many individuals.

- *High*: the feared event affects all individuals.

Table 7.1: BEMS feared events and attributes

Code	Feared Event	Relevant Scenarios	Scale	Irreversibility
FE.1	Excessive data collection	Collection of energy consumption data more frequently than billing period without consumer consent	High	Medium
FE.2	Use of energy consumption data or data inferred from it for unauthorized purpose	Develop detailed consumer profiles, monitoring and restricting energy usage	Medium	Medium
FE.3	Data inference from energy consumption data	Inference about a person's religious beliefs from his energy consumption	Medium	Medium
FE.4	Retaining billing related data more than required	Not deleting energy management suggestions long after consumer stops using utility provider's service, not deleting bills even after 5 years	High	Low
FE.5	Retaining energy consumption data more than required	Ineffective deletion of energy consumption data from utility gateway	High	Low
FE.6	Retaining contact and identification data more than required	Not deleting e-mail address, DoB even after consumer stops using utility provider's service	High	Low
FE.7	Unauthorized access to identification/contact data	Hacker gets access to identification/contact data	Medium	Medium
FE.8	Unauthorized access to billing related data	Hacker gets access to billing data	Medium	Medium
FE.9	Unauthorized access to energy consumption data or data inferred from it	Hacker gets access of data to energy consumption data	Medium	Medium
FE.10	Use of identification/contact data for unauthorized purposes	Targeted advertising	High	Medium
FE.11	Storage and/or use of inaccurate contact/identification data	Sending wrong bill to a consumer due to swapped contact information, inability of consumer to update contact and identification data	Medium	Low
FE.12	Storage and/or use of inaccurate billing data	Charging consumers for inaccurate bills due to wrong bill computation, inability of customer to challenge erroneous bills	Medium	Low
FE.13	Storage and/or use of inaccurate energy consumption data	Charging consumers with inaccurate bills due to inaccurate energy consumption data, inability of customer to challenge erroneous bills	Medium	Low
FE.14	Disclosure of energy consumption data or data inferred from it to unauthorized third parties	Selling energy consumption data to third parties such as insurance providers for financial gain without consumer consent	Medium	High

As for irreversibility, we use the values defined in Table 7.2:

- *Low*: when both the extent of the exposure and the technical difficulty are low or one is low and the other medium.

- *Medium*: when both the extent of the exposure and the technical difficulty are medium or one is low and the other high.

- *High*: when both the extent of the exposure and the technical difficulty are high or one is medium and the other high.

Table 7.2: Values of the irreversibility attribute

Extent of Exposure of Data Due to the Feared Event	Technical Difficulty to Reverse the Effect of the Feared Event	Irreversibility
Low	Low	Low
	Medium	Low
	High	Medium
Medium	Low	Low
	Medium	Medium
	High	High
High	Low	Medium
	Medium	High
	High	High

CHAPTER 8

Privacy Harms

As discussed in the previous chapter, a privacy risk analysis should include, in addition to the evaluation of the likelihood of the feared events, an analysis of their potential impacts in terms of privacy, which we call privacy harms in this book. For example, the disclosure of personal data—a feared event in our terminology—can cause different types of privacy harms such as loss of reputation, financial losses, or psychological harms. We first describe the terminologies used in the literature for privacy harms and sketch the ongoing debate on the nature of privacy harms in Section 8.1. Then we present categories and attributes of privacy harms in Section 8.2 and Section 8.3 respectively and illustrate them with the BEMS System in Section 8.4.

8.1 THE NATURE OF PRIVACY HARMS

Despite the increasing number of cases of privacy breaches reported in the media, with a variety of impacts on the victims, there is still little consensus on the use of the expression "privacy harm" in the literature. Different researchers have used different terms to refer to it or used it with different meanings (such as threats or feared events). It is of prime importance to understand precisely what is covered by the notion of "privacy harm," not only at a conceptual level but also with regard to legal practice. Section 8.1.1 presents these variations on the notion of privacy harm and Section 8.1.2 provides an overview of the ongoing debate about the recognition of privacy harms by law.

8.1.1 VARIATIONS ON PRIVACY HARMS

The notion of privacy harm has been discussed extensively in the legal literature, especially from the point of view of privacy torts [22, 23, 30, 35, 104, 115, 116, 130, 134, 140, 141, 145]. In contrast, computer scientists tend to focus more on threats and feared events [40, 52].

The CIPL report [26] characterizes a privacy harm as *"any damage, injury or negative impact—whether tangible or intangible, economic, non-economic or reputational—to an individual that may flow from the processing of personal data. It extends to any denial of fundamental rights and freedoms."* This characterization is close to the definition of the privacy harm adopted in this book.[1]

---

[1]A privacy harm is defined in Chapter 2 as *"a negative impact of the use of a processing system on a data subject, or a group of data subjects, or society as a whole, from the standpoint of physical, mental, or financial well-being or reputation, dignity, freedom, acceptance in society, self-actualization, domestic life, freedom of expression, or any fundamental right"* (Definition 2.11).

As far as terminology is concerned, Solove [140] seems to use the terms "privacy violation," "privacy harm" and "problems" interchangeably. The CNIL guidelines [32, 33] use the expression "privacy impact" rather than "privacy harm" and define a four-level severity scale for these impacts. Friginal et al. [51, 52] use the term "adverse impact" to refer to the consequences of "threats" and suggest an adverse impact scale, adapted for privacy from the NIST risk assessment guide [17].

The meaning of the notion of "privacy harm" obviously depends on the definition adopted for privacy,[2] which is itself a broad topic of debate going far beyond the scope of this book. Just to take some examples, Solove [138] conceptualizes privacy as a protection against disruptions to certain practices. For example, the invasion of solitude, threats to personal security, the destruction of reputation constitute disruptions of practices. In their pioneering work, Warren and Brandeis [158] referred to privacy in terms of dignitary harms rather than physical injury. They pointed out that the law (in the late 19th century) was beginning to recognize privacy harms other than physical injury, such as mental pain and distress. Risks of bias or discrimination based on knowledge inference should also be considered with great attention, especially at the age of big data. This type of harm, which is discussed by Schwartz and Solove [134], has been termed as *"predictive privacy harm"* by Crawford and Schultz [35].

Calo [22] classifies privacy harms into two categories based on whether the harm is external or internal to the victim. These categories are called *"objective privacy harms"* and *"subjective privacy harms"* respectively.

- *Objective privacy harms* include the non-consensual or unanticipated use of information about a person against that person. The individual does not understand or agree to the particular use of information. For example, a person may, without fully understanding the consequences, reveal personal information on a social network that may later become the basis of rejection of a job application. Objective privacy harms include the misuse of information by human and non-human agents. This is in contrast to the argument that no privacy harm occurs unless a human being sees the information under consideration [61, 79, 117, 121].

- *Subjective privacy harms* originate from the perception of being observed. The notion of "observation" is used here in a broad sense: it could mean watching somebody directly or reading something about them or even drawing inference about them. It can be harm to an individual or to a group and may range in severity from mild discomfort to mental pain and distress. In addition, the mere perception of observation may be sufficient to cause harm. In general, observation may range from casual observation with inhibitive effect on individuals [56] to "dataveillance" [28]. Subjective harms may be acute or ongoing and may occur a long time after the events causing them.

Objective and subjective privacy harms are related to each other. While a subjective harm is the perception of loss of control over data and the fear arising from it, an objective harm may be the actual adverse consequence of this loss of control.

---

[2]For example, Calo characterizes privacy harms as the negative effect of privacy violation [22].

Some scholars [22, 30, 132, 134, 140] argue that privacy harms may affect not only individuals, but also society at large. Harms to society are sometimes referred to as "architectural harm." Power imbalances and interferences with self-actualization of individuals affect the society as a whole and may result from privacy breaches [137]. This type of harm also increase the risk that a person may suffer financial, dignitary or physical harms in the future and can be compared to environmental harms or pollution [140]. According to the notion of constitutive privacy, privacy harms extend beyond the realm of distress caused to individuals and affect society by impeding individual activities that lead to greater social good [140].

A substantial divergence between the different notions of privacy harms considered in the literature is the nature of the stakeholders concerned by the harms. Oetzel and Spiekermann's methodology [106] and the NIST privacy risk management guide [55] consider not only the data subject perspective but also the system operator (data controller) perspective. The main categories of harms for system operators are financial damages and impacts on reputation and brand value. The NIST guide [55] includes impacts such as non-compliance cost, direct cost, reputational cost and internal culture cost. In this book, we focus privacy harms from the perspective of data subjects. An organization may include these harms in its own risk management process but we believe that the two types of risk analyses should not be merged because the interests of data subjects and those of data controllers do not coincide.

8.1.2   RECOGNITION OF PRIVACY HARMS BY LAW

In the previous section, privacy harms were discussed at a conceptual level. A related, and more concrete, viewpoint is the interpretation of the concept in courts and the possibility to get compensations for privacy harms.

In the UK Data Protection Act, a distinction is made between *"substantial damage,"* which refers to financial loss or physical harm, and *"substantial distress,"* which is a *"level of upset, or emotional or mental pain, that goes beyond annoyance or irritation, strong dislike, or a feeling that the processing is morally abhorrent"* [71]. Under this law, a victim can be compensated only if a breach has caused him financial harm or if the distress suffered can be causally linked to the use of data. Laurie et al. [81] argue that this interpretation of the concept of harm is narrow, providing no coverage of psychological or social harms that may result from privacy breaches. They also argue that, since distress is a subjective experience, greater latitude should be given to the subject to decide what constitutes a harm in such situations.

U.S. laws generally consider that victims of harms should get compensation only if there is sufficient evidence to prove that a harm has occurred. More precisely, the harm should be "cognizable," "actual," "specific," "material," "fundamental" or "special" [22, 23]. In *Doe vs. Chao* [154], the U.S. Supreme Court ruled that plaintiffs had to show that they were actually harmed and not just apprehending a harm when their social security numbers were released by the government to unauthorized parties. Legal scholars such as Bartow [15] also express that compelling evidence rather than mere feelings of discomfort and unease is necessary for one to really perceive the intensity of privacy harms.

In reality, it is often difficult to provide such evidence. For example, a person suffering mental distress resulting from the fear of secondary use of information may not be in a good position to plead his case, especially if there is no evidence yet that the information has been misused.

Many scholars stress the fact that privacy harms should also include mental distress, pain, and "injury to the feelings" [158]. Solove [140] provides numerous examples of cases showing how individuals can be harmed physically, mentally, financially and from the standpoint of dignity or reputation because of the release of private information. Physical and financial harms are generally concrete and easy to establish.[3] In contrast, mental distress is often very vague, difficult to measure and equally difficult to substantiate through evidence. As an illustration, too much social control, for example in the form of surveillance, leads to a number of mental distresses: it inhibits freedom of choice, affecting self-determination [78, 132] and causing loss of creativity[4] [30], *chilling effect*,[5] self-censorship [78], embarrassment and damage to reputation and dignity [16, 78]. These harms may be difficult to perceive and prove immediately and may become evident in the longer term, when the impact on society becomes visible.

One of the earliest recognitions of intangible privacy harms can be found in the work of Warren and Brandeis [158]. They stress the lack of a principle, at that time, to consistently deal with injuries to feelings and the painful mental effects. In subsequent works, scholars [22, 23, 139–141] have re-iterated and often criticized the skepticism of courts in their treatment of psychological, structural or intangible privacy harms.

The consequences of the trend of courts to set a higher threshold for privacy harms, as compared to other subjective harms, may often look unfair. A person suffering a severe damage to dignity due to the release of highly personal data is likely to be denied any compensation whereas someone who demonstrates a loss of one dollar from a minor violation can receive a comparatively hefty compensation [23]. Calo [23] also points out that the information industry (e.g., online advertising and data brokerage) is treated as an exception, when, like other multi-billion industries, it creates negative externalities. Privacy harm is one of them—probably the main one—and it should be considered as such by courts.

In this book, we use the term "privacy harm" to encompass both tangible and intangible harms. We take into account all types of harms, whether they can be easily measured or not, substantiated by evidence or not. The cornerstone of a privacy risk analysis is precisely the proper identification of all potential harms and the assessment of their severity, regardless of court practices in terms of compensation.

---

[3]As an example of extreme case, actress Rebecca Schaeffer was murdered in 1989 after the murderer got hold of her home address from the Department of Motor Vehicle records [104, 140].

[4]According to Julie Cohen, *"pervasive monitoring of every first move or false start will, at the margin, incline choices toward the bland and the mainstream"* [30].

[5]Julie Cohen points out that surveillance *"threatens not only to chill the expression of eccentric individuality, but also, gradually, to dampen the force of our aspirations to it"* [30].

Useful inputs to establish the list of relevant harms include previous privacy breaches documented or discussed in the literature, case law and recommendations (e.g., published by Data Protection Authorities such as the CNIL [33]). Last but not least, the most valuable input should be the points of view of the stakeholders. Typically, in the context of a privacy impact assessment, all stakeholders (including representatives of the subjects, e.g., civil liberty associations or privacy advocates) should be consulted and play a key role in the definition of the harms to be considered and the assessment of their level of severity. Needless to say, some subjectivity is unavoidable in this matter. However, all assumptions and choices should be documented and traceable.

8.2   CATEGORIES OF PRIVACY HARMS

Based on the above discussion, we distinguish five broad categories of harms:

1. *Physical harms.* Physical harms include physical injury, ailments and even death. As an example of extreme case, in *Remsburg vs. Docusearch, Inc.* [102], the data subject was murdered at her workplace by a disturbed man who purchased her social security number and employment address from the Docusearch company.

2. *Economic or financial harms.* A person may suffer from damages to his property, financial losses due to fraud, unanticipated payments or debts (e.g., in case of identity theft, or use of bank credentials). For example, in *Armoniene vs. Lithuania*, the disclosure of the HIV-positive status and the extra-marital affair of a person in a daily national newspaper caused the family to leave their village and lose their source of income [81].

3. *Mental or psychological harms.* Mental or psychological distress can be caused, inter alia, by the fear of secondary use of data, the fear of being observed or the fear of loss of control over data. For example, in *Doe vs. Chao* [154], the victims suffered from mental distress due to the fear of secondary use of data when the government released their social security numbers to unauthorized parties.

4. *Harm to dignity or reputation.* The revelation of certain private facts can lead to the loss of dignity and reputation by exposing the data subject to embarrassment or humiliation. For example, in *Roberson vs. Rochester Folding Box Co.* [103], the data subject complained that the appearance of her picture in an advertisement flyer led her to be the subject of humiliation by people who had recognized her face.

5. *Societal or architectural harms.* As discussed above, persistent monitoring and social control can cause a chilling effect, reduce creativity, affect freedom of speech and in the long run impede civic life, artistic and technological innovations [22, 127].

It should be clear that privacy breaches may generally lead to different types of harms. For example, in *Joan W. vs. City of Chicago* [152], the victim complained that Chicago's invasive strip search policy caused her a loss of dignity (harm of category 4). As a consequence, she was under emotional distress which led to reduced socializing, poor performance at work and depression (harm of category 3).

8.3   ATTRIBUTES OF PRIVACY HARMS

In this section, we discuss a set of attributes of privacy harms that should be considered in a privacy risk analysis. These attributes characterize respectively the victims of the harm, the extent of its impact and its severity. We describe each of these attributes in detail in the next sections.

As noted by Ohm [116], the perception of society may change over time and what is considered as a harm today may no longer be considered so in the future (and vice versa). In addition, what is perceived as a harm in one society or country may not be considered as a harm in another society or country. Therefore, the attributes presented here should always be evaluated in context and, as discussed above, in close interaction with all stakeholders.

8.3.1   VICTIMS

The victims are the persons affected by the harm. They can be individuals, groups or society as a whole.

1. *Individuals.* The individuals who are primarily affected by a privacy breach are obviously the data subjects whose personal data have been used in an unauthorized or unexpected way. However, it is often the case that other individuals are also concerned because the data indirectly provides information about them. This is the case for example for location information (e.g., home address), social relationship information or genetic data.

2. *Special Groups.* Certain groups of individuals may be more vulnerable to certain privacy harms than others [81]. For example, Allen [2] states that *"Women face special privacy problems in cyberspace because there, too, they are considered as inferiors, ancillaries, and safe targets and held more accountable for their private conduct."* Women face more risks of being stalked or harassed, both online and offline. Women may also suffer from interferences in their decision on whether or not to terminate her pregnancy.[6] Other groups such as gay or transgender people may be the victims of privacy harms. For example, in *B. vs. France*, the victim suffered mental distress because she had to constantly reveal her identity as a transsexual to third parties. Children represent another group presenting specific privacy risks. For example, they can become victims of sexual predators when they reveal too much information about themselves online.

Last, but not least, some harms, based on profiling, may affect groups that are not socially defined. For example, different treatments can be applied to people visiting certain websites, exhibiting certain behaviors, showing certain interests, using certain kinds of devices,

---

[6]The U.S. Constitution forbids the government from banning the use of contraceptive by married couples. In *Roe vs. Wade*, the court held that the right to privacy encompasses a woman's decision whether or not to terminate her pregnancy.

etc. These harms may be even more difficult to demonstrate than discriminations against constituted social groups.

3. *Society.* As discussed above, harms to society (architectural harms) should also be considered in a privacy risk analysis, even if it is difficult to assess them because they are generally longer term. In fact, a privacy harm may affect some individuals or groups in the short term and society as a whole in the long term. For example, the generalization of video-surveillance systems or tracking devices can lead to a chilling effect which can in the long term be detrimental to democratic life. Harms to society, in general, have deeper roots than individual harms, and feared events may be just one of several causes of such harms.[7]

8.3.2   EXTENT

Generally speaking, the *extent* of a harm characterizes the way the harm affects the lives of the victims. It is the key attribute to assess the *severity* of the harm. The two main components of the extent attribute are the *significance* of the impacts and the *recovery*, which characterizes the capacity of the victims to overcome them.

The impacts can be numerous and of unequal significance, ranging from small inconveniences (e.g., occasional spams) to major impacts (loss of job, divorce, depression, etc.). An impact becomes even more critical when the victims cannot overcome it (or are very unlikely to be able to recover): this is the case, for example, for lifelong disability, loss of family ties and death. The extent is independent of the harm categories presented in Section 8.2 and major (respectively minor) impacts can be of a physical, psychological, reputational, financial or societal nature.

Harms that cannot be perceived immediately or cannot be measured or proved easily should not be underestimated. In addition, harms can be direct or indirect. For example, a tangible harm can lead to an intangible harm or vice versa. As an illustration, identity theft may lead to financial losses as a direct effect, which in turn, may lead to mental distress as an indirect effect. In many cases, victims claim that mental distress caused by a feared event leads to poor work performance which, in turn, may lead to financial losses. The apprehension of a harm can also constitute a harm in itself. The fear that released data could be used for secondary purposes may cause mental distress. The apprehension of being observed may lead to a chilling effect.

Under the *loss of chance doctrine* in the medical sector,[8] the harm can be the deprivation of the chance to survive or to achieve a more favorable medical outcome [165]. Some privacy harms may be looked upon similarly, even if they are difficult to prove. For example, when a student is denied an education loan based on credit record analysis, he may claim to suffer from the lost opportunity of pursuing quality education.

---

[7]Other causes may be corruption, faltering trust in institutions, social inequalities, etc.
[8]The loss of chance doctrine originated in the context of medical malpractice cases where a doctor's negligence deprived a plaintiff of some chances of survival.

8.3.3   SEVERITY

The evaluation of the severity of the risks is one of the main goals of a data protection impact assessment, as set forth in Recital 84 of the GDPR:

"In order to enhance compliance with this Regulation where processing operations are likely to result in a high risk to the rights and freedoms of natural persons, the controller should be responsible for the carrying-out of a data protection impact assessment to evaluate, in particular, the origin, nature, particularity and severity of that risk."

As discussed above, the significance of the impacts and the capacity of the victims to overcome them should be the key factors to take into account in the assessment of the severity of a harm. As an illustration, the CNIL report [33] provides a list of typical privacy harms and a generic description of their impacts with a severity scale mostly based on these two factors. Depending on the situation, other parameters can also be taken into account in the severity assessment (such as the nature of the victims and the risk sources for example). However, as discussed above, privacy harm catalogues and evaluation rules should only serve as general guidelines. In practice, the severity should be evaluated in close interaction with all stakeholders to ensure that the specificities of each situation are properly taken into account.

8.4   ILLUSTRATION: THE BEMS SYSTEM

A number of privacy harms with broadly varying likelihoods and degrees of severity have already been identified in the smart grid literature (see Table 8.1 for a list of examples). They include:

1. Physical harms.

2. Financial harms.

3. Psychological harms.

4. Harms to reputation or dignity.

5. Social or architectural harms.

The attributes for the most relevant harms for the BEMS System are shown in Table 8.2. They are based on the following assumptions for the values of the *significance* and *recovery* attributes.

Significance is measured along the following scale:

- *Low*: victims face very few consequences of the harm with marginal impacts on their lives.

- *Medium*: victims face moderate consequences of the harm with some impact on their lives.

- *High*: victims face significant consequences, with major impacts on their lives.

Table 8.1: Information revealed by Smart Meters and Associated Harms [20, 36, 39, 94, 98, 122]

Harm	Category of the Harm	Information Revealed by Smart Meters	Pattern
Burglary	Financial, psychological	Periods of time when residents are usually away from home	High/low power usage during the day
		Protection of the home by an electronic alarm system	Appliance activity matching alarm system signature
Kidnapping, stalking, child abuse	Physical, financial, psychological	Periods of time when a child is alone at home	Single person power usage or simultaneous power usage at distinct areas of the house during the day
		Protection of the home by an electronic alarm system	Appliance activity matching alarm system signature
		Number of residents in the house	Single person power usage or simultaneous power usage at distinct areas of the house during the day
Profile-based discrimination,[9] disclosure of personal habits	Financial, psychological, harm to reputation/dignity	Presence of expensive gadgets in the house	Appliance activity matching signature of expensive gadgets
		Appliances on when residents are away from home	Appliance activity matching signature of different appliances
		Residents at home all day watching TV or using their computers	Appliance activity matching signature of TV, computer
		Cooking patterns (frequency, time)	High/low power events around meal times for microwave, cook tops, etc.
Surveillance	Psychological, societal, reputation/dignity	Energy consumption for non-essential purposes (e.g., entertainment)	Appliance activity matching signature of television, music systems, etc.

[9] Examples include: increase in insurance premium by health insurance providers based on whether residents use their treadmill everyday or eat outside frequently or by home insurance providers based on how long, how frequently residents are away from home, etc.; less favorable commercial conditions, impact on job or loan applications, etc. [39].

Table 8.2: BEMS harms and their attributes

Code	Example of Harm	Categories	Significance	Recovery	Severity
H.1	Kidnapping of a child	Psychological, financial, physical	High	High	Maximum
H.2	Burglary	Financial, Psychological	Medium	Low	Limited
H.3	Restriction of energy usage	Psychological	Medium	Medium	Significant
H.4	Profile-based discrimination	Psychological, financial	Medium	Medium	Significant

Recovery is measured along the following scale:

- *Low*: victims can easily or quickly recover from the harm.

- *Medium*: victims can recover from the harm but after some time or difficulties.

- *High*: victims can hardly recover (or cannot recover at all) from the harm.

Table 8.3: Significance scale

Significance	Examples
Low	Minor physical ailments, receipt of unsolicited mails, targeted advertising
Medium	Serious physical ailments, restrictions in energy usage, burglary, profile-based discrimination
High	Death, kidnapping of a child, major physical ailments

Based on the *significance* and *recovery* values, the severity of a harm can be evaluated as follows (Table 8.4):

- *Negligible*: when both factors (significance and recovery) are low.

- *Limited*: when one of the factors is low and the other medium.

- *Significant*: when both the factors are medium or one high and the other low.

- *Maximum*: when both factors are high or one high and the other medium.

Needless to say, this simple rule is indicative only and can be adjusted on a case by case basis.[9]

---

[9]Provided, however, that the rules used are clearly defined and their application is documented.

Table 8.4: Calculation rule for the severity attribute

Recovery	Significance	Severity
Low	Low	Negligible
	Medium	Limited
	High	Significant
Medium	Low	Limited
	Medium	Significant
	High	Maximum
High	Low	Significant
	Medium	Maximum
	High	Maximum

CHAPTER 9

Privacy Risk Analysis

In the previous chapters, we have presented and discussed the attributes of the main components of a privacy risk analysis (PRA). In this chapter, we turn our attention to the use of these ingredients in a PRA process. Considering that a PRA should be part of a more general Privacy Impact Assessment (PIA) and PIAs have received a lot of attention during the last decade, we start with an introduction to PIAs in Section 9.1. To make the presentation more concrete, we describe in Section 9.2 the Data Protection Impact Assessment (DPIA) template proposed by the Expert Group 2 of the Smart Grid Task Force mandated by the European Commission [49], which is one of the most comprehensive PIA document currently available. Then we take a more general perspective and provide in Section 9.3 an overview of privacy risk analysis in existing frameworks. In Section 9.4, we build on this review of previous works to present a list of key tasks of a PRA process with their inputs and outputs. We illustrate the last phase of the analysis with the evaluation of the risks for the BEMS System in Section 9.5.

9.1 SCOPE AND OBJECTIVES OF A PIA

Wright and De Hert [162] define PIA as: *"a methodology for assessing the impacts on privacy of a project, policy, programme, service, product or other initiative which involves the processing of personal information and, in consultation with stakeholders, for taking remedial actions as necessary in order to avoid or minimize negative impacts."* Other definitions of PIA used in different countries [29] are presented in Table 9.1. Most of them stress that a PIA should be used to mitigate privacy risks. Some of them focus on compliance while others emphasize that the scope of a PIA should be broader and address all privacy impacts.[1]

The origin of the concept of PIA dates back to the early seventies [29]. Its two main precursors are "technology assessments," which were promoted in particular by the Office of Technology Assessment (OTA) of the U.S. Congress, and "impact statements," which were applied originally in the area of environmental protection. For example, Environmental Impact Statements (EIS) became a requirement for major projects in the U.S. in order to control their negative impacts on the environment. Some of the limitations of EIS, such as insufficient control and audits, were addressed by the concept of Environmental Impact Assessment. In the privacy area, the earliest references to PIA also date back to the seventies but their true development started in the nineties.

---

[1]This is made clear, for example, in the definition used in Alberta: *"The process is designed to ensure that the public body evaluates the project or initiative for technical compliance with the FOIP Act and also assesses the broader privacy implications for individuals."*

Table 9.1: Definitions of privacy impact assessment (PIA) [29]

Country	Definition of Privacy Impact Assessment
New Zealand	A PIA is defined as "*a systematic process for evaluating a proposal in terms of its impact upon privacy.*"
Canada	PIAs "*provide a framework to ensure that privacy is considered throughout the design or re-design of a programme . . . [and to] identify the extent to which it complies with all appropriate statutes.*" This is done to "*mitigate privacy risks and promote fully informed policy.*"
Australia	A PIA is an "*assessment of actual or potential effects of privacy, and how they can be mitigated.*"
New South Wales	"*A PIA involves a comprehensive analysis of the likely impacts of a project upon the privacy rights of individuals. It is a little . . . like an environmental impact assessment done for a new development proposal. The assessment can ensure that any problems are identified—and resolved—at the design stage. PIA is not only about ensuring compliance with the relevant information privacy laws (such as the PPIP Act and the HRIP Act), but can also help to minimize the risk of reputational damage by identifying broader privacy concerns (such as bodily or territorial privacy impacts).*"
Alberta	"*A privacy impact assessment (PIA) is a process that assists public bodies in reviewing the impact that a new program, administrative process or practice, information system or legislation may have on individual privacy. The process is designed to ensure that the public body evaluates the project or initiative for technical compliance with the FOIP Act and also assesses the broader privacy implications for individuals. A PIA is both a due diligence exercise and a risk-management tool. The PIA process requires thorough analysis of the potential impact of the initiative on privacy and a consideration of measures to mitigate or eliminate any negative impact. The PIA is an exercise in which the public body identifies and addresses potential privacy risk that may occur in the course of its operations.*"
United States	"*A PIA is an analysis of how information in identifiable form is collected, stored, protected, shared, and managed . . . [to] ensure that system owners and developers consciously incorporated privacy protection throughout the entire life cycle of a system.*"

It was at this time also that countries such as Canada, New Zealand and Australia started promoting PIAs.

The EU Directive [47] refers to the notion of risk in several places[2] but does not explicitly mandate or even mention the notion of PIA. The situation is very different with the new GDPR [48] in which PIAs play a pivotal role. To be precise, the GDPR uses the term *Data Protection Impact Assessment (DPIA)* rather than Privacy Impact Assessment, but presumably with the same meaning even though this issue has been debated.[3] The GDPR makes DPIAs mandatory in certain situations (Article 35, Paragraph 1):

"Where a type of processing in particular using new technologies, and taking into account the nature, scope, context and purposes of the processing, is likely to result in a high risk to the rights and freedoms of natural persons, the controller shall, prior to the processing, carry out an assessment of the impact of the envisaged processing operations on the protection of personal data."

It also provides an explicit (but not exhaustive) list of cases where a DPIA has to be conducted:

"A data protection impact assessment referred to in paragraph 1 shall in particular be required in the case of:

(a) a systematic and extensive evaluation of personal aspects relating to natural persons which is based on automated processing, including profiling, and on which decisions are based that produce legal effects concerning the natural person or similarly significantly affect the natural person;

(b) processing on a large scale of special categories of data referred to in Article 9(1),[4] or of personal data relating to criminal convictions and offences referred to in Article 10;[5] or

(c) a systematic monitoring of a publicly accessible area on a large scale."

The GDPR also defines the main components of a DPIA:

"The assessment shall contain at least:

(a) a systematic description of the envisaged processing operations and the purposes of the processing, including, where applicable, the legitimate interest pursued by the controller;

(b) an assessment of the necessity and proportionality of the processing operations in relation to the purposes;

(c) an assessment of the risks to the rights and freedoms of data subjects referred to in paragraph 1; and

---

[2]For example, in Article 17 about the security of processing: *"Having regard to the state of the art and the cost of their implementation, such measures shall ensure a level of security appropriate to the risks represented by the processing and the nature of the data to be protected,"* and in Article 20 stating that *"Member States shall determine the processing operations likely to present specific risks to the rights and freedoms of data subjects and shall check that these processing operations are examined prior to the start thereof."*

[3]For example, Wright argues that the expression Data Protection Impact Assessment restricts the type of privacy risks covered by the GDPR, excluding types of privacy such as the privacy of the body, communications privacy, location privacy and the privacy of behaviors [160]. Article 35 may seem a bit ambiguous to this respect, referring to *"assessment of the impact of the envisaged processing operations on the protection of personal data,"* which may seem restrictive, but also to *"risk to the rights and freedoms of natural persons,"* which is broader and seems to cover all potential privacy risks.

[4]Personal data revealing racial or ethnic origin, political opinions, religious or philosophical beliefs, or trade-union membership, and the processing of genetic data, biometric data for the purpose of uniquely identifying a natural person, data concerning health or data concerning a natural person's sex life or sexual orientation.

[5]Personal data relating to criminal convictions and offences or related security measures.

(d) the measures envisaged to address the risks, including safeguards, security measures and mechanisms to ensure the protection of personal data and to demonstrate compliance with this Regulation taking into account the rights and legitimate interests of data subjects and other persons concerned."

The function of a regulation is not to define precisely the details of a PIA though. Before delving into a more general presentation of existing PIA and PRA frameworks, we present in the next section, as a concrete example, the DPIA template proposed by the Expert Group 2 of the Smart Grid Task Force mandated by the European Commission [49].

9.2 DPIA TEMPLATE FOR SMART GRID AND SMART METERING

In order to provide guidance for the deployment of smart metering and smart grid systems in the electricity and gas sectors, the European Commission (EC) issued a recommendation in 2012 for the adoption of a specific DPIA template by Member States [11]. This template was developed by the Expert Group 2 (EG2) with feedbacks from the Working Party 29 [11, 12]. This DPIA template consists of the following eight phases:

1. The goal of the first phase is to determine if a DPIA is at all necessary and who should conduct it. The decision is based on the following criteria:

   (a) *Personal data involved.* It is necessary to determine what personal data are collected and processed by the system, where the expression "personal data" is used in the same sense as in the EU Directive [47]. Processing of personal data should be done only if it is absolutely necessary.

   (b) *Roles of data controller and data processor.* The stakeholders playing the roles of data controller and data data processor should be clearly defined. Again, the terms "data controller" and "data processor" have the same definitions as in the EU Directive.

   (c) *Impact on rights and freedom.* It is necessary to determine whether the data processing could lead to specific risks to the rights and the freedom of the data subjects because of its nature, scope or purpose. If so, a DPIA should be conducted.

   (d) *Timing and motivation.* Ideally, a DPIA should be carried out when the system is conceived, before the design and implementation phases. However, it may also be necessary to perform a DPIA in other situations, for example when the system has undergone substantial modifications, when new types of personal data are to be processed or after the occurrence of privacy breaches. Generally speaking, a DPIA should be performed as early as possible to reduce risks and to avoid costly re-design tasks.

   (e) *Nature of system or application.* The perimeter of the system and its components should be precisely defined to ensure that the objectives and limitations of the DPIA are well understood.

(f) *Legal basis and public concern.* The legal basis of the processing should be made explicit and duly justified. Certain types of processing, such as consumer profiling for targeted advertisements, require user consent, whereas others, such as fraud detection, do not.

(g) *Other criteria.* Other justifications for performing a DPIA, if any, should be identified.

The outcome of this step is a documented conclusion explaining whether a DPIA is necessary or not.

2. The second phase, referred to as *initiation*, is mostly organizational. It includes the definitions of:

(a) *The purpose (objective).* Different stakeholders or members of the organization may pursue different objectives with the DPIA. These objectives must be made clear. For example, the management may be interested in knowing whether an investment would be realistic, whereas system developers may be more interested in the measures to be taken to mitigate risks.

(b) *Team.* A team to execute the DPIA must be formed. Overall, the team should have enough expertise in different fields such as risk assessment, IT architecture and system engineering, information security, privacy and data protection, law, project management and organizational design.

(c) *Resources.* A number of inputs are required to carry out a DPIA. They can be obtained through interviews or from existing documents such as project reports, system design documentation or service provider contracts.

3. The third phase is a preparatory stage for the risk identification phase. It consists of a complete and comprehensive description of the system,[6] its design, environment, boundaries and the data to be processed. Components can be categorized into primary assets (data and processes), which are the focus of the protection, and secondary assets (actors, hardware, software, etc.), which play a role in the management of the primary assets (and therefore also need to be protected).

4. The fourth phase is the identification of all relevant feared events, the corresponding "threats"[7] (which may involve malicious actions such as software alteration or function creep, and exploitation of privacy weaknesses such as insufficient access controls) as well as the risk sources that may cause these feared events.

5. The fifth phase is the risk assessment phase where the impacts of the feared events and the likelihoods of the threats are combined to obtain the levels of risk. The impact of a feared event is obtained from the "level of identifiability" of the data and the "prejudicial effect"

---

[6]For example, using data flow diagrams.
[7]Harm scenarios in our terminology.

of the feared event. The level of identifiability measures how easy it is to identify the data subjects from the data being processed, whereas the prejudicial effect refers to the extent of the damage caused by the feared event. The likelihood of a threat is assessed from the level of vulnerability[8] of the supporting assets and the capabilities of the risk sources such as, inter alia, skills, available time, motivation and financial resources. All attributes take a value in the set {*negligible, limited, significant, maximum*}. Risks can then be prioritized according to their severity and likelihood.

6. The objective of the sixth phase is to determine whether additional controls must be implemented to address the risks identified in the fifth phase. Controls may be technical (privacy enhancing technologies, equipment protection, etc.), organizational (access control procedures, accountability measures, etc.) or legal. The DPIA report must specify how each risk is addressed and whether the controls are sufficient to reduce them to an acceptable level. When a risk is shared with a third party, the report should specify what measures have been taken by the third party to address the risk. Generally speaking, several approaches can be followed to manage risks, including (1) risk modification by the implementation of new controls, (2) risk retention or acceptance if it falls within the acceptance criteria, (3) risk avoidance, which may entail the decision to stop the project, and (4) risk sharing with a third party that can manage the risk more effectively and reduce it to acceptable limits. These approaches are not mutually exclusive and any combination of actions can be adopted to suitably address each risk.

7. The seventh phase is the treatment of the residual risks, that is to say the remaining risks after the implementation of the controls decided in the sixth phase. In this crucial step, the system owner must decide whether additional controls need to be implemented to address the residual risks, especially if their level is still unacceptable. It may happen that the system owner decides to accept a residual risk even if its level remains above the acceptability threshold, but this type of decision needs to be properly justified in the DPIA report by demonstrating that the utility of the corresponding processing far outweighs the risks involved. If all risks have been identified and reduced to acceptable levels, then the system can be implemented. If the system is already in production at the time of carrying out the DPIA, then a specific corrective action plan may need to be implemented in order to remedy the identified risks.

8. In the eighth phase, all the findings of the DPIA and the final results must be documented to facilitate the implementation of the process and to provide evidence to the Data Protection Authority whenever needed. It must be ensured that all undertakings arising from the DPIA process are carried out, including the implementation of required controls and the preparation of a review report. The review report should be presented to the senior manage-

---

[8]Privacy weaknesses in our terminology.

ment and made publicly available. Finally, it is also necessary to assess the need for further DPIAs after a certain period of time or after completion of a new stage of the project.

9.3   PRIVACY RISK ANALYSIS IN EXISTING FRAMEWORKS

In this section, we provide an overview of some PIA and PRA frameworks in order to show their contributions in terms of privacy risk analysis. This discussion is not exhaustive and focuses on the most recent and up-to-date works on PIA and PRA. In the presentation of the works discussed here, we respect the specific terminology used by their authors and make the correspondence with the terminology of this book when necessary. Contributions in this area fall into three main categories:

1. Works [39, 40, 52] that focus almost entirely on PRA and are less concerned about other aspects of PIAs.

2. Works [70, 108–110, 112–114, 161] covering the overall PIA process, but without providing specific details about the PRA phase. These works put more emphasis on the organization and management phases.

3. Works [32, 33, 55, 107] that also cover the whole PIA process, but still provide a good level of detail about the PRA phase. The Expert Group 2 DPIA template presented in the previous section falls into this category.

In the remainder of this section, we first outline some aspects of the overall PIA process as described in the works of categories 2 and 3 above. Next, we describe the PRA steps as defined by works belonging to categories 1 and 3.

PIA Frameworks

The PIAF (Privacy Impact Assessment Framework) project has produced an extensive review of existing PIA processes and methodologies [70, 108–110, 112–114] and proposed a sixteen-step optimized PIA process [161]. When compared to the EG2 document [49], the overall description of this process is at a higher level, focusing on the objectives and requirements of each step rather than on the way to accomplish them. This PIA process can be used as a guideline to conduct organizational and management tasks such as PIA team formation, preparation of a PIA plan, agreement on budget, identification of the stakeholders, consultation of these stakeholders, third party review and accountability. It also includes more technically oriented steps such as the definition of information flows, the analysis of privacy impacts and the identification of risks, but they are not presented in detail. For example, the process provides that risks should be assessed for their likelihood and consequences but it does not specify how this assessment should be done (i.e., what may contribute to the assessment of the likelihood or the consequences). Neither does it go into any detail about the description of the system, feared events, threats or vulnerabilities. Wright [161] stresses the importance of the identification of the project stakeholders, including all parties that may be affected by the technology (e.g., data subjects, regulatory authority, citizen advocacy groups, service providers, manufacturers) so that they can be adequately consulted during the PIA process. He also suggests that the range and the number of the stakeholders to be consulted should be a function of assumptions about the potential privacy risks, their frequency, consequences and the number of people who may be affected.

In comparison with the PIAF framework, the CNIL and the NIST propose higher-level views with less emphasis on stakeholders consultation. The CNIL methodology [32] relies on a four-phase iterative risk management framework consisting of:

1. The definition of the *context* of the processing (including the personal data involved, their lifecycle, supporting assets, retention period, recipients and the processing itself).

2. The definition of existing or planned *controls* (with a clear distinction between controls whose goal is to address privacy risks and mandatory controls, which are necessary to comply with the law, regardless of risks, such as data minimization measures, implementation of information and consent, etc.).

3. The assessment of privacy *risks* (including the definition of risk sources, feared events, threats[9] and the assessment of the likelihood and severity of the risks).

4. The risk management *decisions* (which may lead either to reiterate the process or to prepare an action plan to implement the controls).

Similarly, the NIST guideline [55] defines four broad categories of processes: (1) framing business objectives and organizational privacy governance, (2) assessing system design, and privacy risks, (3) designing privacy controls and (4) monitoring change.

In general, a preliminary step in a PIA process consists in establishing whether a PIA is necessary at all,[10] which is referred to as the *initial analysis* [49] or the *threshold analysis* [161]. This preliminary step, which corresponds to the first phase of the DPIA template presented in Section 9.2, may also lead to the decision to perform a small-scale or a large-scale PIA [70, 107]. Indeed, it is useful to be able to adapt the level of detail required in a PIA [107] so as to avoid the burden of a large-scale PIA process when it is not justified, especially for small and medium-sized companies [70, 107]. Last but not least, all PIA frameworks and recommendations stress that privacy impact assessment should be a continuous improvement and adaptation process.

Privacy Risk Analysis Methods
The core of a PRA is the assessment of the level of risk arising from each feared event. This level of risk is generally characterized by a pair consisting of:

---

[9]Harm scenarios in the terminology of this book.

[10]This is in line with Article 35 of the GDPR, which states that *"where a type of processing in particular using new technologies, and taking into account the nature, scope, context and purposes of the processing, is likely to result in a high risk to the rights and freedoms of natural persons, the controller shall, prior to the processing, carry out an assessment of the impact of the envisaged processing operations on the protection of personal data."* This wording implies that a pre-PIA should be conducted to decide upon the necessity of a full-fledged PIA.

- the likelihood of the feared event and

- the severity of its negative impacts on data subjects.

The GDPR also refers to these two criteria in several places.[11]

The CNIL methodology defines a risk as a feared event with all the threats that may allow it to occur. The likelihood of a threat depends on the level of vulnerability[12] of the supporting assets, the capacities of the risk sources to exploit them and the controls (countermeasures) addressing these vulnerabilities. The likelihood of a feared event is equal to the maximum of the likelihoods of its associated threats.[13] The severity level of a feared event depends on its potential impacts. The CNIL templates and knowledge bases [33] include a scale that can be used to assess privacy impacts. The magnitude of the impacts and the possibility for the victims to overcome them are key factors to assess their severity. The impacts are classified into three broad categories, physical, material and moral, and the severity levels are "negligible," "limited," "significant" and "maximum."

An alternative method for risk assessment is proposed by Cortez and Friginal [105]. One of their goals is to make the assessment as objective as possible through the use of impact and likelihood scales decomposed into four dimensions. The dimensions of the impact scale are the following:

1. The accuracy of the information (which can be coarse-grained or fine-grained).

2. The linkability between pieces of information (which can be easy or complex).

3. The persistence (or duration) of the impact.

4. The dissemination of the information (from limited to public exposure).

Each dimension is assigned a level ("low" or "high") and an overall score is calculated based on these four levels. For example, considering the extreme cases, the impact scale is assigned a score of 0 if all dimensions have level "low" and 10 if all dimensions have level "high."

The dimensions of the likelihood scale are the following:

1. The resources required for the attack.[14]

2. The complexity of the attack.

3. The spatial constraints (whether the attack can be performed remotely or from a specific location only).

---

[11]For example in Recital 76: *"The likelihood and severity of the risk to the rights and freedoms of the data subject should be determined by reference to the nature, scope, context and purposes of the processing."*
[12]Privacy weakness in the terminology of this book.
[13]Considering that the actuation of any of these threats is sufficient to bring about the feared event.
[14]The harm scenario in our terminology.

4. The duration of the observation (whether a single observation is sufficient or multiple observations are necessary).

As for the impact scale, each dimension is assigned a level ("low" or "high") and an overall score is calculated based on these four levels.

For both scales, the authors provide rules to map the different combinations of "high" and "low" levels to quantitative scores. Finally, attack trees can be used to represent the different ways to bring about a feared event and likelihoods can be propagated through the trees to compute the levels of risk. Attack trees are generalized to "harm trees" in [39] to account for the specific nature of privacy risk analysis (as compared to security analysis) and the need to fully integrate privacy harms in the analysis.

The LINDDUN framework [40, 166] relies on the use of data flow diagrams (DFD) to specify the processing system. DFDs are composed of four types of elements: processes, data flows, data stores and external entities. Threat categories[15] are associated with each type of element. For each element affected by a threat category, a list of concrete threats is defined and represented using threat trees. Threat trees also define the pre-conditions (referred to as vulnerabilities[16]) required for the threat to materialize. The LINDDUN framework provides a catalogue of threat tree patterns that can be used by the analyst but does not specify any specific risk assessment method. The framework also provides a guide for the choice of mitigating strategies and techniques to address the threats.

Another important step in a PRA is the presentation of the results of the analysis. Estimated risks may be plotted on a two-dimensional map showing the severity and the likelihood of each risk (or feared event) [32, 33, 49]. The risk map can be decomposed into four sections to improve readability:

1. Risks with high severity and likelihood, which should be considered with the highest priority.

2. Risks with a high severity but low likelihood, which deserve special attention.

3. Risks with low severity but high likelihood, which also merit special consideration.

4. Risks with low severity and likelihood, which are more likely to be deemed acceptable.

Another option, which may turn out to be too reductive in practice, consists in expressing the level of risk as a single value. For example, the NIST [55] suggests the computation of the risk as a product of the likelihood of a problematic data action[17] by the impact of this action.

---

[15]LINDDUN uses the following threat categories: linkability, identifiability, non-repudiation, detectability, information disclosure, content unawareness, policy and consent noncompliance, which, incidentally, have inspired the name "LINDDUN."
[16]Privacy weaknesses in the terminology of this book.
[17]Feared event in the terminology of this book.

9.4 KEY STEPS OF A PRIVACY RISK ANALYSIS

In this section, we build on the review of the previous works and the definitions introduced in the previous chapters to suggest a list of key steps that should be part of any PRA framework. We do not attempt to describe the implementation of each of these steps, which can be more or less complex and vary among the frameworks, but rather define their inputs, outputs and objectives:

1. *Definition of the system.* Depending on the context of the risk analysis (objectives of the analysis, level of development of the system, etc.), the definition can be more or less precise (Chapter 3). It should include at least the purpose of the system, the specification of its functionalities, its interactions with its environment (inputs and outputs), its internal data flows and the existing or planned privacy protection measures. The description can be made in a more or less formal way (from a natural language to semi-formal[18] or formal[19] models).

2. *Definition of the personal data.* The type of personal data processed by the system can be derived from the output of Step 1 if it is sufficiently precise. To the extent possible, each category of data should be associated with its relevant attributes as defined in Chapter 4. All categories of data should be considered, including metadata and personal data collected implicitly.

3. *Definition of the stakeholders.* Data subjects, data controllers and data processors concerned by the system should be identified as well as potential third parties, as suggested in Chapter 5.

4. *Definition of the risk sources.* All the risk sources should be considered, including insiders (e.g., employees of the data controller) and risk sources related to the data subjects (e.g., acquaintances, friends and family) as discussed in Chapter 6. Their attributes should be defined as precisely as possible as they strongly influence the likelihood of the harm scenarios.

5. *Analysis of the privacy weaknesses of the system.* The determination of the privacy weaknesses requires an expert analysis of the system as defined in Step 1. When the system is available, it may also be useful to experiment it (e.g., through penetration testing or re-identification attempts).

6. *Definition of the feared events.* The feared events can be derived from the privacy weaknesses and/or the privacy harms because they are in an intermediate position: they are made possible (or facilitated) by privacy weaknesses and they lead to privacy harms. Depending on the initial knowledge and intuitions of the analyst, a top-down approach (from harms to feared events), a bottom-up approach (from privacy weaknesses to feared events) or an iterative approach can be followed.

---

[18]For example using graphical notations.
[19]Formal means mathematical here, for example through the use of logical frameworks or dedicated specification languages.

7. *Definition of the relevant harms and assessment of their severity level.* All possible harms should be considered, including individual and collective harms. Their severity level can take a value in a list of pre-defined qualitative values such as "negligible," "limited," "significant" and "maximum." These levels should be defined as precisely as possible to ensure a common understanding and a uniform interpretation of the results of the analysis. Their assessment can rely on existing tables or catalogues or result from calculations based on attributes such as significance and recovery, as explained in Chapter 8. In the context of a PIA, the determination of the harms and their severity levels should result from interactions with the stakeholders. These interactions may also lead to reconsider the outcomes of the previous steps, in particular the definition of the personal data (Step 2) and the risk sources (Step 4), typically when some risk factors have been overlooked.

8. *Determination of the harm scenarios and their likelihood.* In order to define the harm scenarios, the experts need to consider the privacy weaknesses of the system, the risk sources and the feared events (which are the outcomes of the harm scenarios). The basic question to address is: how can privacy weaknesses be exploited by risk sources to bring about feared events? The likelihood of a harm scenario depends on its complexity (especially the difficulty to exploit the privacy weaknesses of the system) and the attributes of the risk sources (motivation, resources, etc.). The likelihood of a harm depends on the likelihood of the harm scenarios that can lead to this harm. As discussed in Section 9.3, different approaches can be followed to establish the harm scenarios and their likelihood. Dedicated techniques can also be devised for specific harm scenarios such as de-anonymization.

9. *Presentation of the risks.* The importance of the presentation of the results of the analysis should not be underestimated. Indeed, it is on the basis of this presentation that the first decisions about the system are likely to be taken. Ideally, it should be possible to get first a broad view of all risks with their likelihood and severity (e.g., through a two-dimensional map), and then to obtain further details about specific risks (e.g., through harm trees[20]).

10. *Decision and choice of countermeasures.* The last step is the decision-making stage, which involves high-level decisions, such as risk acceptance, transfer or mitigation and more technical decisions concerning appropriate countermeasures. Many privacy enhancing techniques are available, which can be applied in different contexts [59, 60, 76, 85–87, 90, 119, 129, 143]. Generally speaking, [83] distinguishes four types of privacy enhancing technologies to enforce data minimization (respectively for communication services, access services, computation services and the exploitation of databases) and four types of techniques to enhance control over personal data (respectively decision support, consent, enforcement and accountability). Catalogues of countermeasures are also proposed by the CNIL [31] and in the LINNDUN framework [40, 166] and systematic approaches have

---

[20]Or attack trees or threat trees.

been proposed to implement privacy by design [4, 5]. A review of technical countermeasures and privacy by design is beyond the scope of this book. The interested reader can find an up-to-date review of privacy enhancing technologies in [83].

Different frameworks may recommend conducting the above steps in different orders and put more or less emphasis or provide more or fewer details on each of them. For example, as discussed above, the sets of privacy weaknesses, feared events and harms are strongly interconnected and an iterative approach is often necessary to reach satisfactory definitions. Needless to say, the entire process itself should in general be iterative. For example, when the decision has been taken to include additional countermeasures, it is necessary to re-evaluate the risks to confirm that they have been reduced to an acceptable level.

Appendix D shows how some of the above steps are covered by existing PIA and PRA frameworks.

9.5   ILLUSTRATION: EVALUATION OF THE RISKS FOR THE BEMS SYSTEM

In this section, we illustrate Step 8 (determination of the harm scenarios and their likelihood) of the privacy risk analysis with the BEMS System. We also provide some hints on Step 9 (presentation of the risks) and Step 10 (design and choice of countermeasures).

A harm may result from different combinations of feared events. For example, profile-based discrimination can happen if sufficiently fine-grained energy consumption data is collected, inferences about personal habits or lifestyle are drawn from these data and the results of such inferences are sold to third parties without consumer consent. Similarly, a privacy weakness may facilitate multiple feared events. For example, if the utility provider does not enforce sufficient accountability measures (e.g., system audits), excessive collection of data and their use for unauthorized purposes are more likely to occur (because they are more likely to remain undetected). As discussed above, a natural way to represent these complex relationships between harms, feared events and privacy weaknesses is through harm trees [39]. The root node of a harm tree represents a harm, leaf nodes represent the exploitation of privacy weaknesses by risk sources, and intermediate nodes are feared events, connected by AND or OR nodes.

For example, the harm tree pictured in Figure 9.1 expresses the fact that profile-based discrimination[21] may happen in case of excessive collection of energy consumption data (FE.1, as defined in Chapter 7), data inference (FE.3) and use of energy consumption data for unauthorized purposes, either by a hacker (FE.9), by the utility provider itself (FE.2) or by third parties that have received the data from the utility provider (FE.14). Excessive data collection may happen when the data controller does not ensure data minimization (V.11), does not allow consumers to opt out from such data collection (V.12) and does not have sufficient system audit in place (V.14). Similarly, Figure 9.2 shows the harm tree for the burglary harm (H.2). Dotted lines in the trees

---

[21]Examples include: increase in insurance premium by health insurance providers, less favorable commercial conditions, etc.

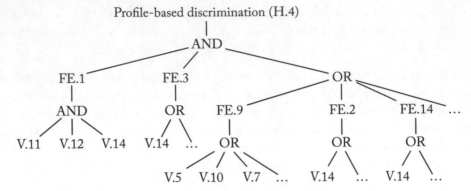

Figure 9.1: Harm tree for profile-based discrimination (H.4).

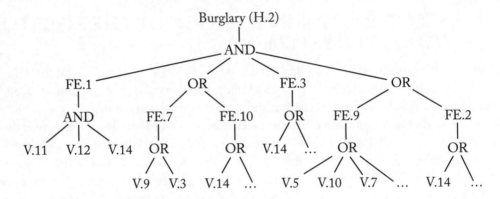

Figure 9.2: Harm tree for burglary (H.2).

represent the fact that there may be other feared events or other privacy weaknesses that are not pictured for the sake of conciseness and are ignored here.

Harm trees are useful for the calculation of the likelihood of the risks. The analyst may begin by defining the ease of exploitation of each privacy weakness for each type of risk source based on their attributes. The likelihood of each harm can then be computed based on the harm trees, using the attributes of the risk sources which are the most likely to exploit each privacy weakness.

The calculation of the likelihoods can be done using qualitative values (based on a fixed scale of levels such as "negligible," "limited," "significant," "maximum," as discussed above) or quantitative values (e.g., probabilities). While probabilities may be difficult to estimate for input values[22] and difficult to grasp by decision makers, symbolic values are sometimes too fuzzy and

---

[22]For example the likelihood of exploitation of a privacy weakness by a risk source.

may lead to different interpretations. We choose a combined approach here, with qualitative input values that are converted into quantitative values for processing based on the harm trees and converted back into qualitative values for the final output (likelihood of the harm). We emphasize however, that the analyst can choose different representations, provided that they are properly documented and justified. This process is illustrated for the discrimination harm in Figure 9.3.

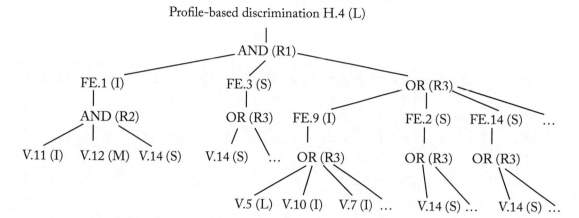

Figure 9.3: Computation of likelihood of profile-based discrimination (H.4).

We use the following correspondence between qualitative values and quantitative values p:

1. *Negligible (N)* for $p \leq 0.01\%$;

2. *Limited (L)* for $0.01\% < p < 0.1\%$;

3. *Intermediate (I)* for $0.1\% < p \leq 1\%$;

4. *Significant (S)* for $1\% < p \leq 10\%$;

5. *Maximum (M)* for $p > 10\%$.

The computations of likelihoods based on the harm trees rely on the following rules,[23] where P is the likelihood of a node and P_i is the likelihood of its ith child node:

R1. AND node with independent child nodes: $P = \prod_i P_i$;

R2. AND node with dependent child nodes[24]: $P = Min_i(P_i)$, i.e., the minimum of the likelihoods of the child nodes;

---

[23]The rules are applied bottom-up.
[24]In order to err on the safe side in terms of privacy protection, we consider dependent nodes such that one node may imply another node.

R3. OR node with independent nodes: $P = 1 - \prod_i (1 - P_i)$;

R4. OR node with dependent nodes[25]: $P = Min(1, \sum_i P_i)$, i.e., the sum of the likelihoods of the child nodes if this sum is less than one, and one otherwise.

As for likelihood scales, different choices can be made provided they are justified and traceable.

Table 9.2: Privacy weaknesses of the BEMS system

Code	Privacy Weaknesses
V.1	Security vulnerability in PMS
V.2	Security vulnerability in MDMS
V.3	Security vulnerability in CIS
V.4	Functional errors in PMS
V.5	Functional errors in MDMS
V.6	Functional errors in CIS
V.7	Unencrypted energy consumption (per meter ID) data processing
V.8	Unencrypted billing related data processing
V.9	Unencrypted consumer identification and contact data processing
V.10	Unencrypted transmission of energy consumption data from home appliance to smart meter
V.11	Non-enforcement of data minimization
V.12	No opt-outs for consumers for high volume/precision data collection
V.13	Not assigning capabilities to consumers to challenge erroneous data about themselves
V.14	Insufficient system audit

As discussed in Chapter 8, the relevant harms and their severity should ideally be determined in collaboration with the stakeholders. A first assessment of the severity of a harm can still be made using the *significance* and *recovery* attributes as discussed in Chapter 8. Based on these attributes, the level of severity derived for the discrimination and burglary harms were respectively *Significant* and *Limited* (Table 8.2 in Chapter 8).

The risk level of each harm can then be represented as a pair consisting of its severity and likelihood. Figure 9.3 shows that, based on the assumptions made on the exploitability of the privacy weaknesses, the likelihood of Harm H.4 (profile-based discrimination) is *Limited*. The

---

[25]In order to err on the safe side in terms of privacy protection, we consider dependent nodes such that each node may exclude the other nodes.

same calculation yields the result *Negligible* for Harm H.2 (burglary).[26] Therefore, the risk levels for the two harms considered here are respectively:

- Discrimination harm (H.4):

    - Severity = *Significant*
    - Likelihood = *Limited*

- Burglary harm (H.2):

    - Severity = *Limited*
    - Likelihood = *Negligible*

The risk level for the discrimination harm is thus higher than the risk level of the burglary harm. The risk levels for other harms can be computed in the same way and the decision makers are then in a position to decide which risks are acceptable and which ones should be mitigated.

The analysis of all harm trees corresponding to harms whose risk level is above the acceptability threshold also reveal privacy weaknesses that have the strongest impact on the overall privacy risks. This information helps the analyst decide which privacy weaknesses should be mitigated first. For example, Fig. 9.1 and Fig. 9.2 reveal that V.11, V.12 and V.14 are necessary conditions for the occurrences of the both harms. Mitigating them should therefore be a high priority. In addition, V.14 is the most commonly occurring privacy weakness, meaning that strong efforts should be put into accountability measures (especially auditing).

Many techniques have been proposed to enhance privacy in smart metering and smart grid systems [1, 18, 19, 27, 34, 45, 54, 73, 77, 80, 84, 89, 91, 95, 123, 125, 126, 168]. The analyst can refer to existing catalogues or state of knowledge papers, such as [74], which reviews the protocols and privacy enhancing technologies available for smart grids and analyses their features. As an illustration, several solutions are available enhance data minimization (addressing V.11). One of them relies on local calculations of the bills based on certified readings output by a tamper-evident meter [125]. Zero-knowledge proofs are used to prove to the utility provider that the calculations are correct without leaking any additional information. This solution makes it possible to keep the benefits of smart meters in terms of billing (pay-per-use) while protecting customers' privacy since only the required information is known by the utility provider (the amount of the bill). Energy management suggestions could also be computed locally, which would make it possible to enjoy all the functionalities of the BEMS System without disclosing any consumption data (except through the bills) to the utility provider. The use of this kind of protocol has a major impact on the whole architecture of the processing system though. Hence the importance to conduct PIAs and PRAs as early as possible in the life cycle of a system.

---

[26]The computation of these likelihoods is based on the rules presented in this chapter. The expert has to choose input values (likelihood of exploitation of privacy weaknesses) lying within the intervals indicated at the leaf nodes. The choice of these values relies on the expert's assessment of the exploitability of the privacy weaknesses. We assume that the following values were chosen for the calculations of Figure 9.3: V.5: **0.001**; V.7: **0.002**; V.10: **0.002**; V.11: **0.01**; V.12: **0.15**; V.14: **0.1**.

CHAPTER 10

Conclusion

In this book, we have focused on privacy risk analysis (PRA) considered as the technical core of privacy impact assessment (PIA). We have mentioned, without going into detail, the other (mostly organizational) aspects of PIAs which are already well documented and discussed in the literature. Computer security is another strongly connected area that we have not covered as such in this book because security risk analysis is a well established area that has already given rise to a significant body of literature, standards and certification schemes [82]. Privacy is sometimes seen as a subfield of computer security from the technical point of view but this position does not stand up to analysis, unless we want to take a very restrictive vision of the concept of the privacy. Indeed, many key aspects of privacy such as data minimization, purpose specification, use limitation, consent or control over personal data, do not pertain to traditional computer security. As an illustration, security is just one of the eight principles of the OECD Privacy Principles.[1]

In fact, the relationships between privacy and computer security are varied and subtle. First, the aim of privacy is not to protect resources or businesses, but people: hence the importance of privacy impacts (harms), which can concern individuals, groups or society as a whole. In addition, a privacy risk analysis should take the point of view of the data subject. As a result, the data controller itself should be considered as a source of risk—sometimes even the main source of risk—and the very functionality of the system can constitute a privacy weakness.[2] For these reasons, in this book we used the expressions "risk source," "privacy weakness" and "harm scenario" rather than "adversary," "vulnerability" and "attack" which are more common in computer security.

As far as controls are concerned, privacy protection can rarely be achieved by hiding data mechanisms only (or by preventing access to data) because data processing is supposed to have a utility. The challenge is rather to find different ways to organize the computation, for example by moving from centralized to distributed architectures, or using techniques such as homomorphic encryption or zero-knowledge proofs, which make it possible to perform computations while minimizing the disclosure of data. Accountability measures can also play a key role when *a priori* controls are not possible or sufficient and should be supplemented by *a posteriori* controls. Needless to say, privacy protection strongly relies on the use of appropriate security techniques (such as encryption or access control) and security and privacy are often mutually reinforcing, but there are also cases where security requirements can be in tension with privacy protection. For example,

---

[1] oecdprivacy.org
[2] For example, in the case of video-surveillance systems or location-based services.

security logs, which are necessary to support intrusion detection, can also create new privacy risks (when they contain personal data or make it possible to derive personal information).

Taking a global perspective, the high-level processes followed in computer security risk analysis and privacy risk analysis are very similar though. For example, the four-phase iterative risk management framework[3] recommended by the CNIL is directly inspired by the EBIOS security risk analysis framework [32] and the process proposed by the NIST [55] is not significantly different. Organizations should therefore be able to integrate security and privacy risk analysis frameworks, for example with the results of the security risk analysis provided as input assumptions to the privacy risk analysis, and possible iterations of the whole process.

The goal of this book was both to provide a state of the art and to lay the foundations for a more rigorous approach to PRA. We have suggested a terminology, proposed classifications for the key factors that have to be considered in a PRA and defined the requirements of the main steps of the analysis. The requirements suggested here can be fulfilled in most contexts in the current state of technologies but further research is still needed in several directions. A striking example is the assessment of the guarantees provided by anonymization algorithms and their mitigating effect on privacy risks. Indeed, in order to allow data analytics while preserving privacy, the first strategy consists in anonymizing datasets. However, anonymization often comes into conflict with the objective of preserving the utility of the data, and the parties interested in their exploitation can be tempted to use light anonymization techniques to preserve this utility. In addition, the fact that a piece of data is anonymous is by essence relative because it depends on the amount of auxiliary knowledge available to the risk source. This background knowledge may itself depend on many factors, in particular the level of exposure of the subject in the media or the existence of public information (such as voting registers). Technically speaking, a variety of theoretical anonymization metrics have been proposed in the literature [42, 44, 53] but it is not obvious to integrate them in a PRA to provide practical assessments of the residual risks of de-anonymization in specific situations. Other areas such as cloud computing in which a variety of stakeholders are usually involved also deserve further work [3].

It should also be stressed that the results of a risk analysis can never provide absolute guarantees because they depend on a number of assumptions (e.g., on risk sources, privacy weaknesses, harm severity, etc.) that may be challenged or may need to be reconsidered after a period of time. Therefore, PRAs and PIAs should be renewed periodically and also in the occurrence of any event that could change some of these assumptions (e.g., privacy breach, availability of new background data, or new technological developments).

A PRA should lead to the application of a set of appropriate measures, justified by the results of the analysis and the potential benefits of the processing. These measures can include, in addition to the application of technical controls, any useful organizational and legal measures (e.g., physical access control, awareness measures, non disclosure agreements, etc.). In order to increase

---

[3]The four steps are respectively: (1) the definition of the context of the processing; (2) the definition of existing or planned controls; (3) the assessment of privacy risks; and (4) the risk management decisions (Chapter 9).

the benefits of a PRA, it would also be useful to establish more formal links between privacy risks and potential countermeasures. These links could be used to provide suggestions to the decision makers or to the designers of the system. Generally speaking, more tools are needed to support PRA. PIA environments have already been developed [3, 118, 144] but they mostly focus on the organizational aspects and the collection of all useful information from the stakeholders, usually through the use of interactive questionnaires. More support on the technical parts would also be welcome, including the systematic construction of harm trees based on privacy weaknesses and the evaluation of the likelihood and severity of privacy harms.

Last but not least, in addition to the help in the decision making process, the key benefit of a risk analysis is in terms of accountability and continuous improvement: because it makes it possible to trace all assumptions and motivations for each decision, it contributes to the general accountability and transparency principles which are promoted by most privacy and data protection regulations [21].

Summary of Categories and Attributes of the Components of a Privacy Risk Analysis

Table A.1: PRA components: types and attributes (*Continues.*)

Components	Categories	Attributes

Data	1. Identication data
	2. Economic and financial information
	3. Health information
	4. Genetic information
	5. Behavioral information
	6. Technical data
	7. Location data
	8. Contact information
	9. Information about professional life
	10. Information about one's origin
	11. Information about personal life
	12. Judicial information
	13. Information about personal belief
		1. Related to nature of data
		  (a) Sensitivity
		  (b) Uniqueness
		2. Related to data format
		  (a) Representation
		  (b) Form
		  (c) Precision
		  (d) Volume
		3. Related to context
		  (a) Origin
		  (b) Purpose
		  (c) Retention
		4. Related to control
		  (a) Visibility
		  (b) Intervenability

System	✗	1. Functional specication 2. Interface 3. Data flows 4. Supporting assets 5. Actors

Table A.1: (*Continued.*) PRA components: types and attributes

Components	Categories	Attributes
Stakeholders	1. Data subject 2. Data controller 3. Data processor 4. Third parties	1. Relationships 2. Communications
Risk sources	1. Data subject 2. Data controller 3. Data processor 4. Third parties	1. Nature 　(a) Type 　(b) Relationships 2. Motivation 　(a) Incentives 　(b) Disincentives 3. Resources 　(a) Background information 　(b) Access rights 　(c) Tools and skills 　(d) Computational power
Feared events	1. Data collection 2. Data access 3. Data modification 4. Data usage 5. Data inference (including re-identification) 6. Data disclosure (including publication and dissemination) 7. Data retention	1. Scale 2. Irreversibility 3. Harm Scenarios 4. Likelihood
Privacy harms	1. Physical harms 2. Economic or financial harms 3. Societal or architectural harms 4. Mental or psychological harms 5. Harms to dignity or reputation	1. Victims 　(a) Individual 　(b) Special groups 　(c) Society 2. Extent 　(a) Signicance 　(b) Recovery 3. Severity

APPENDIX B

Definitions of Personal Data Across Regulations and Standards

Table B.1: Definitions of personal data and PII (*Continues.*)

Reference	Definition
EU Directive 95/46/EC [47]	Personal data shall mean any information relating to an identified or identifiable natural person ("data subject"); an identifiable person is one who can be identified, directly or indirectly, in particular by reference to an identification number or to one or more factors specific to his physical, physiological, mental, economic, cultural or social identity. In order to determine whether a person is identifiable, one must take into account all the means *likely reasonably* to be used either by the controller or by any other person to identify the said person.
ISO/IEC 29100:2011 [72]	Personally identifiable information is any information that (a) can be used to identify the PII principal to whom such information relates, or (b) is or might be directly or indirectly linked to a PII principal. To determine whether a PII principal is identifiable, account should be taken of all the means which can reasonably be used by the privacy stakeholder holding the data, or by any other party, to identify that natural person.
French Act No. 78-17 of 6 January 1978 on Information Technology, Data Files and Civil Liberties [50]	Personal data means any information relating to a natural person who is or can be identified, directly or indirectly, by reference to an identification number or to one or more factors specific to him. In order to determine whether a person is identifiable, all the means that the data controller or any other person uses or may have access to should be taken into consideration.

Table B.1: (*Continued.*) Definitions of personal data and PII

Reference	Definition
Children's Online Privacy Protection Act (U.S.) [146]	Personal information is individually identifiable information about an individual collected online, including first and last names, home address, e-mail address, telephone number, Social Security Number or any combination of information that permits physical or online contact.
Song-Beverly Act (California, U.S.) [149]	Personal identification information is information concerning the cardholder, other than information set forth on the credit card, and including, but not limited to, the cardholder's address and telephone number.
Gramm-Leach-Bliley Act of 1999 (U.S.) [147]	Defines personally identifiable financial information as non-public personal information. It fails to define the term "non-public." The term may mean information not found in the public domain. The FTC Regulations to GLBA explains the term in detail but still leaves confusion as to whether some publicly applicable information can be considered as non-public for the purposes of the statute. The applicable regulations take into consideration any information that a consumer provides on a financial application which dilutes the core statutory concept of non-public.[4]
NIST [92]	Personally identifiable information is any information about an individual maintained by an agency, including (1) any information that can be used to distinguish or trace an individual's identity, such as name, social security number, date and place of birth, mother's maiden name or biometric records; and (2) any other information that is linked or linkable to an individual, such as medical, educational, financial and employment information.
[4] See Schwartz and Solove [135], pg. 889.	

APPENDIX C

Definitions of Stakeholders Across Regulations and Standards

Table C.1: Definitions of stakeholders (*Continues.*)

Reference	Definition
ISO/IEC 29100:2011 [72]	**PII controller:** Privacy stakeholder(s) that determines the purposes and means for processing personally identifiable information other than natural persons who use data for personal purposes. A PII controller sometimes instructs others (e.g., PII processors) to process PII on its behalf while the responsibility for the processing remain with the PII controller. **PII principal:** Natural person to whom the PII relates. Depending on the jurisdiction and the particular data protection and privacy legislation, the synonym "data subject" can also be used. **PII processor:** Privacy stakeholder that processes PII on behalf of and in accordance with the instructions of a PII controller.
EU Directive 95/46/EC [47]	**Controller:** The natural or legal person, public authority, agency or any other body which alone or jointly with others determines the purposes and means of the processing. **Processor:** A natural or legal person, public authority, agency or any other body which processes personal data on behalf of the controller. **Third party:** Any natural or legal person, public authority, agency or any other body other than the data subject, the controller, the processor and the persons who, under the direct authority of the controller or the processor, are authorized to process the data. **Data subject:** Identified or identifiable natural person to whom the data relates.

Table C.1: (*Continued.*) Definition of stakeholders (*Continues.*)

Reference	Definition
French Act No. 78-17 of 6 January 1978 [50]	**Data subject:** The data subject of a processing of personal data means an individual to whom data covered by the processing relate. **Data controller:** It means, unless expressly designated by legislative or regulatory provisions relating to this processing, a person, public authority, department or any other organization who determines the purposes and means of the data processing.
Children's Online Privacy Protection Act (U.S.) [146]	**Child/Children:** An individual (individuals) under the age of 13. **Operator:** Any person who operates a website located on the Internet or an online service and who collects or maintains personal information from or about the users of, or visitors to, such a website, or on whose behalf such information is collected or maintained where the website or online service is used for commercial purposes.
Song-Beverly Credit Card Act (California, U.S.) [149]	**Card issuer:** Any person who issues a credit card or the agent of that person for that purpose with respect to the credit card. **Cardholder:** A natural person to whom a credit card is issued for consumer credit purposes, or a natural person who has agreed with the card issuer to pay consumer credit obligations arising from the issuance of a credit card to another natural person. For purposes of some sections of the act, the term includes any person to whom a credit card is issued for any purpose, including business, commercial or agricultural use, or a person who has agreed with the card issuer to pay obligations arising from the issuance of that credit card to another person. **Retailer:** Every person other than a card issuer who furnishes money, goods, services or anything else of value upon presentation of a credit card by a cardholder. It does not mean the state, a county, city, city and county or any other public agency.
Health Information Portability and Accountability Act (U.S.) [148, 150]	**Health care clearinghouse:** A public or private entity that processes or facilitates the processing of nonstandard data elements of health information into standard data elements. **Health care provider:** This term includes a provider of services, a provider of medical or other health services and any other person furnishing health care services or supplies.

Table C.1: (*Continued.*) Definition of stakeholders

Reference	Definition
Video Privacy Protection Act of 1988 (U.S.) [151]	**Patron:** Any individual who requests or receives (A) services within a library; or (B) books or other materials on loan from a library. **Consumer:** Any renter, purchaser or subscriber of goods or services from a video tape service provider. **Video Service Provider/Library:** (A) any publicly owned library open to general public; (B) any library in a primary, secondary, or post-secondary education institution (i) that is a public institution; or (ii) any part of which receives federal financial assistance; (C) any person or other entity engaging in a business that includes the renting or selling of prerecorded video tapes or similar audiovisual materials that (i) operates in or affects interstate or foreign commerce; or (ii) is supplied with video tapes to rent or sell through distributors that operate in interstate or foreign commerce; (D) any person or other entity to whom a disclosure is made but only with respect to the information contained in that disclosure; or (E) any person acting as an agent of an entity described above but only with respect to information obtained from such entity.

APPENDIX D

Privacy Risk Analysis Components in Existing Frameworks

Table D.1: Definitions of processing systems

PIA Proposal	Definition of the Processing System
EG 2's DPIA (SGTF) [49]	• In terms of primary[5] and supporting assets.[6] • Use of data flow diagrams.
Cortez and Friginal. [105]	Describes privacy risk assessment with respect to location-based services.
CNIL [32, 33]	In terms of personal data, processes, supporting assets[7] and controls.[8]
Wright [161]	Includes contextual information, information flow description (purpose, storage, security, processing, distribution of personal data), etc.
NIST PIA [55]	Describes lifecycle of data actions[9] and specific contextual factors that may increase or decrease the risk potential of the data actions.
PIA for RFID [106, 107]	• Includes detailed description of scenarios and use cases, system components, interfaces, data flows and the parties involved. • Identifies scope, boundaries and assets (resources and information) to be protected.
Deng et al. [40]	Describes system in terms of data flows, data stores, processes and external entities; uses data flow diagram.

[5] Processes, personal data.
[6] Hardware, software, network, people, etc.
[7] Information systems (hardware, software etc.) and organizations (people, paper documents, paper transmission channels).
[8] Legal and risk-treatment controls.
[9] Data actions are information system operations that process personal information.

Table D.2: Definitions of personal data

PIA Proposal	Definition of the Personal Data
EG 2's DPIA (SGTF) [49]	Includes the level of identfiiability of personal data.[10]
Cortez and Friginal [105]	Includes accuracy[11] and linkability[12] of information.
CNIL [32, 33]	• Various types[13] of personal data. • Includes level of identifiability of personal data.[14]
Wright [161]	Identification of what information is collected during information flow description.
NIST PIA [55]	Personal information associated with each data action are identified at a granular level.
PIA for RFID [106, 107]	Denition of privacy target.[15]
Deng et al. [40]	• Included within system description. • Includes unlinkability of information pieces, confidentiality and anonymity of data, content awareness of personal data, etc.

[10] Assigned levels: negligible, limited, significant, maximum.

[11] Geographical or temporal accuracy, assigned high for fine-grained and low for coarse-grained levels.

[12] Low linkability if it is complex to relate one information with another, high otherwise.

[13] Common personal data, personal data perceived as sensitive, etc.

[14] Assigned levels: negligible, limited, significant, maximum.

[15] Privacy targets include ensuring the legitimacy of processing, quality, security of personal data, etc.

Table D.3: Definitions of stakeholders

PIA Proposal	Definition of the Stakeholders
EG 2's DPIA (SGTF) [49]	Need to clarify who are the data controllers and data processors.
Cortez and Friginal [105]	✗
CNIL [32, 33]	✗
Wright [161]	Identication of data controllers[16] and data subjects[17] during information flow description.
NIST PIA [55]	✗
PIA for RFID [106, 107]	✗
Deng et al. [40]	✗

[16] Who will collect data.
[17] From whom data will be collected.

Table D.4: Definitions of risk sources

PIA Proposal	Definition of the Risk Sources
EG 2's DPIA (SGTF) [49]	Description of risk sources[18] during risk identification.
Cortez and Friginal [105]	Aims to provide better understanding of attack goals and attacker profiles.
CNIL [32, 33]	Description of risk sources[19] and their capabilities during risk identification.
Wright [161]	✗
NIST PIA [55]	✗
PIA for RFID [106, 107]	✗
Deng et al. [40]	The adversary model depends on the system trust boundary.

[18] Insider, outsider, non-human.

[19] Internal and external human sources and non-human sources.

Table D.5: Definitions of privacy weaknesses

PIA Proposal	Definition of the Privacy Weakness
EG 2's DPIA (SGTF) [49]	Level of vulnerability estimated[20] for each threat.
Cortez and Friginal [105]	✗
CNIL [32, 33]	Level of vulnerability estimated[21] for each threat.
Wright [161]	✗
NIST PIA [55]	✗[22]
PIA for RFID [106, 107]	✗
Deng et al. [40]	Depicted in threat trees as preconditions to threats, exploited for privacy attack scenarios.

[20] Assigned different levels: negligible, limited, significant and maximum.

[21] Assigned different levels: negligible, limited, significant and maximum.

[22] Internal and external human sources and non-human sources.

Table D.6: Definitions of feared events

PIA Proposal	Definition of Feared Events
EG 2's DPIA (SGTF) [49]	Feared events[23] identified during risk identification.
Cortez and Friginal [105]	✗
CNIL [32, 33]	• Feared events[24] identified during risk identification. • The severity of the feared events depends on the prejudicial effects of potential impacts and controls likely to modify them.
Wright [161]	✗
NIST PIA [55]	Definition of problematic data actions.
PIA for RFID [106, 107]	Definition of threats corresponding to each privacy target.
Deng et al. [40]	List of threats: linkability, identifiability, detectability, non-repudiation, information disclosure, content unawareness, policy and consent non-compliance.

[23] Such as unavailability of legal processes, illegitimate access to personal data, change in purpose of processing, unwanted change, disappearance, diverting of personal data.

[24] Such as illegitimate access to personal data, unwanted modification or disappearance of personal data.

Table D.7: Definitions of harms and assessment of their severity level

PIA Proposal	Definition of Harms and Assessment of their Severity Level
EG 2's DPIA (SGTF) [49]	• Impact[25] of feared events[26] on data subjects measured[27] during risk assessment. • Severity = level of identification of personal data + level of prejudicial effects.
Cortez and Friginal [105]	The selection of the value (from a scale of 0 to 10) for impact depends on several factors: accuracy of the information, linkability among information pieces, persistence of the impact and the level of information dissemination.
CNIL [32, 33]	Scale to determine the severity levels[28] of physical, moral and material impacts.
Wright [161]	✗
NIST PIA [55]	Estimation of the potential impact[29] of a problematic data action on the organization.
PIA for RFID [106, 107]	• Defined in terms of degree of protection required for privacy targets. • Assignment of impact levels[30] concerning social standing, reputation, financial well-being, personal freedom of data subject.[31]
Deng et al. [40]	✗

[25] Prejudicial effect.

[26] Instead of privacy harms.

[27] Assigned different levels: negligible, limited, significant and maximum.

[28] Negligible, limited, significant, maximum.

[29] Non-compliance cost, direct cost, reputational cost, internal culture cost.

[30] Low, medium, high.

[31] Also considers impact on reputation and brand value and financial loss of the organization.

Table D.8: Definitions of harm scenarios and their likelihood

PIA Proposal	Determination of Harm Scenarios and their Likelihood
EG 2's DPIA (SGTF) [49]	• Determination of threats leading to feared events during risk identification. • Determination of likelihood of threat = level of vulnerabilities of supporting assets + capabilities of risk sources, during risk assessment. • Risk likelihood is obtained from the likelihood of threats.
Cortez and Friginal [105]	• Likelihood computation depends on the attacker and the attack tree. • Likelihood can be estimated (assigned values between 0 and 10) based on several factors: the resources[32] required by the attack, the exploit complexity[33] required by the attack, the spatial constraints[34] of the attack and the duration[35] of the necessary observation of victim nodes.
CNIL [32, 33]	• Determination of threats leading to feared events during risk identification. • Determination of likelihood of threats based on the vulnerability level of supporting assets, capability level of risk sources and controls likely to modify them, during risk assessment. • Likelihood of the risk is the highest likelihood value of the threats associated with the feared events.
Wright [161]	✗
NIST PIA [55]	Determination of the likelihood of a problematic data action.
PIA for RFID [106, 107]	• Likelihood calculation of threat.[36] • Identification of existing controls help to judge real threats and their likelihood.
Deng et al. [40]	Threat trees reflecting common attack patterns.

[32] Low if low computational power is enough, high otherwise.

[33] Low if the attack is easy to launch, high if profound knowledge is required to execute the attack.

[34] Low if the attack can be performed remotely, high if the attacker must be located at a specific location.

[35] Low if a single observation is enough, high if many observations are required.

[36] Likely or not likely.

Table D.9: Presentation of the risks

PIA Proposal	Presentation of the Risks
EG 2's DPIA (SGTF) [49]	Presented on a risk map.
Cortez and Friginal [105]	Presented as the vector (likelihood, impact).
CNIL [32, 33]	Presented on a risk map.
Wright [161]	✗
NIST PIA [55]	Presented as a product of the likelihood of a problematic data action and the impact of the problematic data action.
PIA for RFID [106, 107]	Threat likelihood expressed as likely (yes) or not likely (no).
Deng et al. [40]	✗

Bibliography

[1] Gergely Ács and Claude Castelluccia. I Have a Dream! (Differentially Private Smart Metering). In *Information Hiding*, pages 118–132. Springer, 2011. DOI: 10.1007/978-3-642-24178-9_9. 79

[2] Anita L. Allen. Gender and Privacy in Cyberspace. *Stanford Law Review*, pages 1175–1200, 2000. DOI: 10.2307/1229512. 56

[3] Rehab Alnemr, Erdal Cayirci, Lorenzo Dalla Corte, Alexandr Garaga, Ronald E. Leenes, Rodney Mhungu, Siani Pearson, Chris Reed, Anderson Santana de Oliveira, Dimitra Stefanatou, Katerina Tetrimida, and Asma Vranaki. A Data Protection Impact Assessment Methodology for Cloud. In *Privacy Technologies and Policy—Third Annual Privacy Forum, APF 2015, Luxembourg, October 7–8, 2015, Revised Selected Papers*, pages 60–92, 2015. DOI: 10.1007/978-3-319-31456-3_4. 1, 82, 83

[4] Thibaud Antignac and Daniel Le Métayer. Privacy Architectures: Reasoning about Data Minimisation and Integrity. In *Security and Trust Management*, volume 8743 of *Lecture Notes in Computer Science*, pages 17–32. Springer, 2014. DOI: 10.1007/978-3-319-11851-2_2. 75

[5] Thibaud Antignac and Daniel Le Métayer. Privacy by Design: From Technologies to Architectures. In *Privacy Technologies and Policy*, volume 8450 of *Lecture Notes in Computer Science*, pages 1–17. Springer, 2014. DOI: 10.1007/978-3-319-06749-0_1. 75

[6] Article 29 Data Protection Working Party. Statement on the Role of a Risk-based Approach in Data Protection Legal Frameworks. Text adopted by the Article 29 Data Protection Working Party on 30 May 2014. xiii

[7] Article 29 Data Protection Working Party. Opinion 04/2007 on the Concept of Personal Data, 2007. 20

[8] Article 29 Data Protection Working Party. Opinion 01/2010 on the Concepts of "Controller" and "Processor", 2010. 6, 36

[9] Article 29 Data Protection Working Party. Opinion 05/2010 on Industry Proposal for a Privacy and Data Protection Impact Assessment Framework for RFID Applications, 2010. 1

[10] Article 29 Data Protection Working Party. Opinion 08/2012 Providing Further Input on the Data Protection Reform Discussions, 2012. 4, 5

[11] Article 29 Data Protection Working Party. Opinion 04/2013 on Data Protection Impact Assessment Template for Smart Grid and Metering Systems ("DPIA Template") prepared by Expert Group 2 of the Commission's Smart Grid Task Force, 2013. 1, 66

[12] Article 29 Data Protection Working Party. Opinion 07/2013 on Data Protection Impact Assessment Template for Smart Grid and Metering Systems ("DPIA Template") prepared by Expert Group 2 of the Commission's Smart Grid Task Force, 2013. 1, 66

[13] Article 29 Data Protection Working Party. Opinion 05/2014 on Anomymisation Techniques, 2014. 22

[14] Ken Barker, Mina Askari, Mishtu Banerjee, Kambiz Ghazinour, Brenan Mackas, Maryam Majedi, Sampson Pun, and Adepele Williams. A Data Privacy Taxonomy. In *Dataspace: The Final Frontier*, pages 42–54. Springer, 2009. DOI: 10.1007/978-3-642-02843-4_7. 26, 36

[15] Ann Bartow. A Feeling of Unease about Privacy Law. *University of Pennsylvania Law Review*, 154, pages 52–63, 2006. 53

[16] Stanley I. Benn. Privacy, Freedom, and Respect for Persons. Pennock, J. R. and Chapman, J. W. (Eds.), *Nomos XIII: Privacy*. Atherton Press, New York, 1971. 54

[17] Rebecca M. Blank and Patrick D. Gallagher. *Guide for Conducting Risk Assessments (NIST Special Publication 800-30 Revision 1)*. National Institute of Standards and Technology, 2012. 8, 52

[18] Rakesh Bobba, Himanshu Khurana, Musab AlTurki, and Farhana Ashraf. PBES: A Policy Based Encryption System with Application to Data Sharing in the Power Grid. In *Proc. of the 4th International Symposium on Information, Computer, and Communications Security*, pages 262–275. ACM, 2009. DOI: 10.1145/1533057.1533093. 79

[19] Jens-Matthias Bohli, Christoph Sorge, and Osman Ugus. A Privacy Model for Smart Metering. In *IEEE International Conference on Communications Workshops (ICC)*, pages 1–5. IEEE, 2010. DOI: 10.1109/iccw.2010.5503916. 13, 79

[20] Ian Brown. Britain's Smart Meter Programme: A Case Study in Privacy by Design. *International Review of Law, Computers and Technology*, 28(2), pages 172–184, 2014. DOI: 10.1080/13600869.2013.801580. 13, 59

[21] Denis Butin and Daniel Le Métayer. A Guide to End-to-End Privacy Accountability. In *1st IEEE/ACM International Workshop on TEchnical and LEgal aspects of data pRIvacy and*

SEcurity, TELERISE, pages 20–25. IEEE/ACM, 2015. DOI: 10.1109/telerise.2015.12. 83

[22] Ryan Calo. The Boundaries of Privacy Harm. *Indiana Law Journal*, 86, pages 1131–1617, 2011. 51, 52, 53, 54, 55

[23] Ryan Calo. Privacy Harm Exceptionalism. *Colorado Technology Law Journal*, 12, pages 361–364, 2014. 51, 53, 54

[24] Ann Cavoukian and Daniel Castro. Big Data and Innovation, Setting the Record Straight: De-identification Does Work. http://www2.itif.org/2014-big-data-deidentifi cation.pdf, 2014. Accessed: 2016-07-13. 23

[25] Ann Cavoukian, Jules Polonetsky, and Christopher Wolf. Smart Privacy for the Smart Grid: Embedding Privacy into the Design of Electricity Conservation. *Identity in the Information Society*, 3(2), pages 275–294, 2010. DOI: 10.1007/s12394-010-0046-y. 13

[26] Centre for Information Policy Leadership (CIPL) Hunton & Williams LLP. A Risk-based Approach to Privacy: Improving Effectiveness in Practice, 2014. xiii, 7, 45, 46, 51

[27] Dong Chen, David Irwin, Prashant Shenoy, and John Albrecht. Combined Heat and Privacy: Preventing Occupancy Detection from Smart Meters. In *IEEE International Conference on Pervasive Computing and Communications (PerCom)*, pages 208–215. IEEE, 2014. DOI: 10.1109/percom.2014.6813962. 79

[28] Roger Clarke. Profiling: A Hidden Challenge to the Regulation of Data Surveillance. *JL and Inf. Sci.*, 4, page 403, 1993. 52

[29] Roger Clarke. Privacy Impact Assessment: Its Origins and Development. *Computer Law and Security Review*, 25(2), pages 123–135, 2009. DOI: 10.1016/j.clsr.2009.02.002. 1, 63, 64

[30] Julie E. Cohen. Examined Lives: Informational Privacy and the Subject as Object. *Stanford Law Review*, pages 1373–1438, 2000. DOI: 10.2307/1229517. 51, 53, 54

[31] Commission Nationale de l'Informatique et des Libertes (CNIL). Measures for the Privacy Risk Treatment, 2012. 74

[32] Commission Nationale de l'Informatique et des Libertes (CNIL). Privacy Impact Assessment (PIA) Methodology (How to Carry Out a PIA), 2015. 5, 8, 19, 27, 35, 41, 43, 45, 52, 69, 70, 72, 82

[33] Commission Nationale de l'Informatique et des Libertes (CNIL). Privacy Impact Assessment (PIA) Tools (templates and knowledge bases), 2015. 8, 9, 19, 26, 27, 41, 42, 52, 55, 58, 69, 71, 72

[34] Gianpiero Costantino and Fabio Martinelli. Privacy-Preserving Energy-Reading for Smart Meter. In *Inclusive Smart Cities and e-Health*, pages 165–177. Springer, 2015. DOI: 10.1007/978-3-319-19312-0_14. 79

[35] Kate Crawford and Jason Schultz. Big Data and Due Process: Toward a Framework to Redress Predictive Privacy Harms. *Boston College Law Review*, 55, pages 93–130, 2014. 51, 52

[36] Colette Cuijpers and Bert-Jaap Koops. Smart Metering and Privacy in Europe: Lessons from the Dutch Case. In *European Data Protection: Coming of Age*, pages 269–293. Springer, 2013. DOI: 10.1007/978-94-007-5170-5_12. 13, 59

[37] Ulrich Dammann. 3 Weitere Begriffsbestimmungen; § 44 Strafvorschriften. *Simitis, Spiros*. 20

[38] Amit Datta, Michael Carl Tschantz, and Anupam Datta. Automated Experiments on Ad Privacy Settings. *Proc. on Privacy Enhancing Technologies*, 2015(1), pages 92–112, 2015. DOI: 10.1515/popets-2015-0007. 4

[39] Sourya Joyee De and Daniel Le Métayer. Privacy Harm Analysis: A Case Study on Smart Grids. In *International Workshop on Privacy Engineering (IWPE)*. IEEE, 2016. 1, 59, 69, 72, 75

[40] Mina Deng, Kim Wuyts, Riccardo Scandariato, Bart Preneel, and Wouter Joosen. A Privacy Threat Analysis Framework: Supporting the Elicitation and Fulfilment of Privacy Requirements. *Requirements Engineering*, 16(1), pages 3–32, 2011. DOI: 10.1007/s00766-010-0115-7. 1, 12, 51, 69, 72, 74

[41] Josep Domingo-Ferrer. A Three-Dimensional Conceptual Framework for Database Privacy. In *Proc. of the 4th VLDB Workshop Secure Data Management (SDM)*, volume 4721, pages 193–202. Springer Science and Business Media, 2007. DOI: 10.1007/978-3-540-75248-6_14. 36

[42] Josep Domingo-Ferrer, David Sánchez, and Jordi Soria-Comas. Database Anonymization: Privacy Models, Data Utility, and Microaggregation-based Inter-model Connections. *Synthesis Lectures on Information Security, Privacy, and Trust*, 8(1), pages 1–136, 2016. DOI: 10.2200/s00690ed1v01y201512spt015. 21, 82

[43] Natasha H. Duarte. The Home out of Context: The Post-Riley Fourth Amendment and Law Enforcement Collection of Smart Meter Data. *NCL Rev.*, 93, page 1140, 2014. 13

[44] Cynthia Dwork. A Firm Foundation for Private Data Analysis. *Communications of the ACM*, 54(1), pages 86–95, 2011. DOI: 10.1145/1866739.1866758. 82

[45] Costas Efthymiou and Georgios Kalogridis. Smart Grid Privacy via Anonymization of Smart Metering Data. In *1st IEEE International Conference on Smart Grid Communications (SmartGridComm)*, pages 238–243. IEEE, 2010. DOI: 10.1109/smartgrid.2010.5622050. 79

[46] Khaled El Emam and Cecilia Alvarez. A Critical Appraisal of the Article 29 Working Party Opinion 05/2014 on Data Anonymization Techniques. *International Data Privacy Law*, 2014. DOI: 10.1093/idpl/ipu033. 22

[47] European Commission. EU Directive 95/46/EC—The Data Protection Directive, 1995. xiii, 4, 5, 19, 24, 29, 35, 36, 65, 66

[48] European Commission. Regulation (EU) 2016/679 of the European Parliament and of the Council of 27 April 2016 on the protection of natural persons with regard to the processing of personal data and on the free movement of such data, and repealing Directive 95/46/EC (General Data Protection Regulation), 2016. xiii, 1, 4, 5, 25, 65

[49] Expert Group 2 of Smart Grid Task Force. Data Protection Impact Assessment Template for Smart Grid and Smart Metering Systems, 2014. 63, 66, 69, 70, 72

[50] French National Assembly. Act no. 78-17 of January 6, 1978 on Information Technology, Data Files and Civil Liberties as amended by French Act No. 2004-801 of August 6, 2004 and by French Act No. 2009-526 of May 12, 2009. 19, 35, 36

[51] Jesús Friginal, Jérémie Guiochet, and Marc-Olivier Killijian. A privacy risk assessment methodology for location-based systems. http://homepages.laas.fr/guiochet/tel echarge/MOBIQUITOUS2013.pdf. Accessed: 2016-07-13. 46, 52

[52] Jesús Friginal, Jérémie Guiochet, and Marc-Olivier Killijian. Towards a Privacy Risk Assessment Methodology for Location-Based Systems. In *Mobile and Ubiquitous Systems: Computing, Networking, and Services*, pages 748–753. Springer, 2014. DOI: 10.1007/978-3-319-11569-6_65. 1, 26, 45, 46, 51, 52, 69

[53] Benjamin C. M. Fung, Ke Wang, Rui Chen, and Philip S. Yu. Privacy-Preserving Data Publishing: A Survey of Recent Developments. *ACM Computing Survey*, 42(4), 2010. DOI: 10.1145/1749603.1749605. 82

[54] Flavio D. Garcia and Bart Jacobs. Privacy-Friendly Energy-Metering via Homomorphic Encryption. In *Security and Trust Management*, pages 226–238. Springer, 2011. DOI: 10.1007/978-3-642-22444-7_15. 79

[55] Michael Garcia, Naomi Lefkovitz, and Suzanne Lightman. *Privacy Risk Management for Federal Information Systems (NISTIR 8062 (Draft))*. National Institute of Standards and Technology, 2015. 2, 8, 9, 53, 69, 70, 72, 82

[56] Ruth Gavison. Privacy and the Limits of Law. *Yale Law Journal*, pages 421–471, 1980. DOI: 10.2307/795891. 52

[57] Raphael Gellert. Data Protection: A Risk Regulation? Between the Risk Management of Everything and the Precautionary Alternative. *International Data Privacy Law*, 5(1), pages 3–19, 2015. DOI: 10.1093/idpl/ipu035. xiii

[58] Raphael Gellert. Understanding Data Protection as Risk Regulation. *Journal of Internet Law*, 18(11), pages 3–15, 2015. xiii

[59] Craig Gentry. Computing on Encrypted Data. In *Proc. of the 8th International Conference on Cryptology and Network Security CANS*, page 477. Springer, 2009. DOI: 10.1007/978-3-642-10433-6_32. 74

[60] Craig Gentry. Fully Homomorphic Encryption using Ideal Lattices. In *Proc. of the 41st Annual ACM Symposium on Theory of Computing, STOC*, pages 169–178. ACM, 2009. DOI: 10.1145/1536414.1536440. 74

[61] Eric Goldman. *Data Mining and Attention Consumption*. Springer, 2006. DOI: 10.1007/0-387-28222-x_13. 52

[62] Eloise Gratton. If Personal Information is Privacy's Gatekeeper, then Risk of Harm is the Key: A Proposed Method for Determining What Counts as Personal Information. *Albany Law Journal of Science and Technology*, 24, pages 105–195, 2013. DOI: 10.2139/ssrn.2334938. 26

[63] James Grimmelmann. Saving Facebook. *Iowa Law Review*, 94(4), pages 1137–1793, 2009. 28, 45

[64] The Smart Grid Interoperability Panel Cyber Security Working Group. *Introduction to NISTIR 7628: Guidelines for Smart Grid Cyber Security*. 2010. 13

[65] Brian Hayes. Uniquely Me! *American Scientist*, 102, March–April 2014. DOI: 10.1511/2014.107.106. 21

[66] Peter Hoath and Tom Mulhall. Hacking: Motivation and Deterrence, Part I. *Computer Fraud and Security*, 1998(4), pages 16–19, 1998. DOI: 10.1016/s1361-3723(97)86611-0. 42

[67] Thomas J Holt and Max Kilger. Examining Willingness to Attack Critical Infrastructure Online and Offline. *Crime and Delinquency*, 58(5), pages 798–822, 2012. DOI: 10.1177/0011128712452963.

[68] Thomas J. Holt and Max Kilger. Know Your Enemy: The Social Dynamics of Hacking. *The Honeynet Project*, pages 1–17, 2012. 42

[69] W Kuan Hon, Christopher Millard, and Ian Walden. Who is Responsible for "Personal Data" in Cloud Computing? The Cloud of Unknowing, Part 2. *International Data Privacy Law*, 2(1), pages 3–18, 2012. DOI: 10.1093/idpl/ipr025. 37

[70] Information Commissioner's Office. Privacy Impact Assessment Handbook, Version 2.0. Cheshire, UK: Wilmslow, 2003. 69, 70

[71] Information Commissioner's Office (ICO) UK. Preventing Processing Likely to Cause Damage or Distress. `https://ico.org.uk/for-organisations/guide-to-data-pr otection/principle-6-rights/damage-or-distress/`. Accessed: 2016-02-05. 53

[72] ISO/IEC.   Information Technology—Security Techniques—Privacy Framework (ISO/IEC 29100:2011), 2011. 19, 35, 36

[73] Marek Jawurek, Martin Johns, and Florian Kerschbaum. Plug-in Privacy for Smart Metering Billing. In *Privacy Enhancing Technologies*, pages 192–210. Springer, 2011. DOI: 10.1007/978-3-642-22263-4_11. 79

[74] Marek Jawurek, Florian Kerschbaum, and George Danezis. Privacy Technologies for Smart Grids—A Survey of Options. Microsoft MSR-TR-2012-119, 2012. 79

[75] Rosemary Jay and Angus Hamilton. *Data Protection Law and Practice*. Sweet & Maxwell, Ltd., 2007. 20

[76] Taeho Jung, Xiang-Yang Li, Zhiguo Wan, and Meng Wan. Privacy Preserving Cloud Data Access with Multi-Authorities. In *Proc. of IEEE INFOCOM*, pages 2625–2633. IEEE, 2013. DOI: 10.1109/infcom.2013.6567070. 74

[77] Georgios Kalogridis, Costas Efthymiou, Stojan Z. Denic, Tim Lewis, Rafael Cepeda, et al. Privacy for Smart Meters: Towards Undetectable Appliance Load Signatures. In *1st IEEE International Conference on Smart Grid Communications (SmartGridComm)*, pages 232–237. IEEE, 2010. DOI: 10.1109/smartgrid.2010.5622047. 79

[78] Jerry Kang. Information Privacy in Cyberspace Transactions. *Stanford Law Review*, pages 1193–1294, 1998. DOI: 10.2307/1229286. 54

[79] Orin S Kerr. Searches and Seizures in a Digital World. *Harvard Law Review*, pages 531–585, 2005. 52

[80] Klaus Kursawe, George Danezis, and Markulf Kohlweiss. Privacy-friendly Aggregation for the Smart-grid. In *Privacy Enhancing Technologies*, pages 175–191. Springer, 2011. DOI: 10.1007/978-3-642-22263-4_10. 79

[81] Graeme Laurie, Leslie Stevens, Kerina H. Jones, and Christine Dobbs. A Review of Evidence Relating to Harm Resulting from Uses of Health and Biomedical Data. Technical report, Report prepared for the Nuffield Council on Bioethics Working Party on Biological and Health Data and the Expert Advisory Group on Data Access, 2014. 46, 53, 55, 56

[82] Daniel Le Métayer. IT Security Analysis: Best Practices and Formal Approaches. In *Foundations of Security Analysis and Design IV (FOSAD), LNCS 4677*. Springer, 2007. DOI: 10.1007/978-3-540-74810-6_3. 81

[83] Daniel Le Métayer. Whom to Trust? Using Technology to Enforce Privacy. In *Enforcing Privacy*, pages 395–437. Springer, 2015. DOI: 10.1007/978-3-319-25047-2_17. 74, 75

[84] Fengjun Li, Bo Luo, and Peng Liu. Secure Information Aggregation for Smart Grids Using Homomorphic Encryption. In *1st IEEE International Conference on Smart Grid Communications (SmartGridComm)*, pages 327–332. IEEE, 2010. DOI: 10.1109/smartgrid.2010.5622064. 79

[85] Ninghui Li, Tiancheng Li, and Suresh Venkatasubramanian. t-Closeness: Privacy Beyond k-Anonymity and l-Diversity. In *IEEE 23rd International Conference on Data Engineering (ICDE)*, pages 106–115. IEEE, 2007. DOI: 10.1109/icde.2007.367856. 74

[86] Yehuda Lindell and Benny Pinkas. Privacy Preserving Data Mining. *Journal of Cryptology*, 15(3), pages 177–206, 2002. DOI: 10.1007/s00145-001-0019-2.

[87] Yehuda Lindell and Benny Pinkas. Secure Multiparty Computation for Privacy-Preserving Data Mining. *Journal of Privacy and Confidentiality*, 1(1), page 5, 2009. DOI: 10.4018/9781591405573.ch189. 74

[88] Mikhail Lisovich, Deirdre K. Mulligan, Stephen B. Wicker, et al. Inferring Personal Information from Demand-Response Systems. *IEEE Security and Privacy*, 8(1), pages 11–20, 2010. DOI: 10.1109/msp.2010.40. 13

[89] Rongxing Lu, Xiaohui Liang, Xu Li, Xiaodong Lin, and Xuemin Sherman Shen. EPPA: An Efficient and Privacy-Preserving Aggregation Scheme for Secure Smart Grid Communications. *IEEE Transactions on Parallel and Distributed Systems*, 23(9), pages 1621–1631, 2012. DOI: 10.1109/tpds.2012.86. 79

[90] Ashwin Machanavajjhala, Daniel Kifer, Johannes Gehrke, and Muthuramakrishnan Venkitasubramaniam. l-diversity: Privacy Beyond k-Anonymity. *ACM Transactions on Knowledge Discovery from Data (TKDD)*, 1(3), 2007. DOI: 10.1145/1217299.1217302. 74

[91] Felix Gomez Marmol, Christoph Sorge, Osman Ugus, and Gregorio Martínez Pérez. Do Not Snoop My Habits: Preserving Privacy in the Smart Grid. *IEEE Communications Magazine*, 50(5), pages 166–172, 2012. DOI: 10.1109/mcom.2012.6194398. 79

[92] Erika McCallister, Tim Grance, and Karen Scarfone. *Guide to Protecting the Confidentiality of Personally Identifiable Information (PII) (NIST Special Publication 800-122)*. National Institute of Standards and Technology, 2010. DOI: 10.6028/nist.sp.800-122.

[93] Patrick McDaniel and Stephen McLaughlin. Security and Privacy Challenges in the Smart Grid. *IEEE Security and Privacy*, 7(3), pages 75–77, 2009. DOI: 10.1109/msp.2009.76. 13

[94] Eoghan McKenna, Ian Richardson, and Murray Thomson. Smart Meter Data: Balancing Consumer Privacy Concerns with Legitimate Applications. *Energy Policy*, 41, pages 807–814, 2012. DOI: 10.1016/j.enpol.2011.11.049. 13, 59

[95] Stephen McLaughlin, Patrick McDaniel, and William Aiello. Protecting Consumer Privacy from Electric Load Monitoring. In *Proc. of the 18th ACM conference on Computer and Communications Security*, pages 87–98. ACM, 2011. DOI: 10.1145/2046707.2046720. 13, 79

[96] Sonia McNeil. Privacy and the Modern Grid. *Harvard Journal of Law and Technology*, 25(1), pages 199–226, 2011. DOI: 10.2139/ssrn.1928254. 13

[97] Carol Meyers, Sarah Powers, and Daniel Faissol. Taxonomies of Cyber Adversaries and Attacks: A Survey of Incidents and Approaches. *Lawrence Livermore National Laboratory*, 7, pages 1–22, 2009. DOI: 10.2172/967712. 42

[98] Andrés Molina-Markham, Prashant Shenoy, Kevin Fu, Emmanuel Cecchet, and David Irwin. Private Memoirs of a Smart Meter. In *Proc. of the 2nd ACM Workshop on Embedded Sensing Systems for Energy Efficiency in Building*, pages 61–66. ACM, 2010. DOI: 10.1145/1878431.1878446. 13, 28, 59

[99] Yves-Alexandre de Montjoye, Cesar A. Hidalgo, Michel Verleysen, and Vincent D. Blondel. Unique in the Crowd: The Privacy Bounds of Human Mobility. *Scientific Reports, Nature*, March 2013. DOI: 10.1038/srep01376. 21

[100] Yves-Alexandre de Montjoye, Laura Radelli, Vivek Kumar Singh, and Alex Sandy Pentland. Unique in the Shopping Mall: On the Reidentifiability of Credit Card Meta Data. *Science 30*, January 2015. DOI: 10.1126/science.1256297. 21

[101] Arvind Narayanan and Edward W. Felten. No Silver Bullet: De-identification Still Doesn't Work, 2014. 23

[102] New Hampshire Supreme Court. *Remsburg v. Docusearch, 149 N.H. 148, 816 A.2d 1001.* 2003. 55

[103] New York Court of Appeals. *Roberson v. Rochester Folding Box Co., 171 N.Y. 538; 64 N.E. 442.* 1902. 55

[104] Helen Nissenbaum. Privacy as Contextual Integrity. *Washington Law Review*, 79(1), pages 119–158, 2004. 7, 28, 51, 54

[105] Miguel Nunez del Prado Cortez and Jesús Frignal. Geo-Location Inference Attacks: From Modelling to Privacy Risk Assessment (Short Paper). In *Dependable Computing Conference (EDCC), 2014 Tenth European*, pages 222–225. IEEE, 2014. DOI: 10.1109/edcc.2014.32. 71

[106] Marie Caroline Oetzel and Sarah Spiekermann. A Systematic Methodology for Privacy Impact Assessments: A Design Science Approach. *European Journal of Information Systems*, 23(2), pages 126–150, 2014. DOI: 10.1057/ejis.2013.18. 2, 11, 12, 46, 53

[107] Marie Caroline Oetzel, Sarah Spiekermann, Ingrid Grüning, Harald Kelter, and Sabine Mull. Privacy Impact Assessment Guideline for RFID Applications, 2011. 1, 2, 69, 70

[108] Office of Management and Budget (OMB). OMB Guidance for Implementing the Privacy Provisions of the E-Government Act of 2002, 2003. 69

[109] Office of the Information Privacy Commissioner of Alberta. Privacy Impact Assessment (PIA) Requirements, 2009.

[110] Office of the Chief Information and Privacy Officer. Privacy Impact Assessment Guide for the Ontario Public Service. Toronto: Queen's Printer for Ontario, 2010. 69

[111] Office of the Consumer Affairs and Business Regulation (OCABR). Requirements for Security Breach Notifications under Chapter 93H. http://www.mass.gov/ocabr/data-privacy-and-security/data/requirements-for-security-breach-notifications.html. Accessed: 2016-07-11. 20

[112] Office of the Privacy Commissioner. *Privacy Impact Assessment Handbook*, 2007. 69

[113] Office of the Privacy Commissioner. *Privacy Impact Assessment Guide*, 2010.

[114] Office of the Victorian Privacy Commissioner (OVPC). Privacy Impact Assessments—A Guide for the Victorian Public Sector, 2009. 69

[115] Paul Ohm. Broken Promises of Privacy: Responding to the Surprising Failure of Anonymization. *UCLA Law Review*, 57, pages 1701–1819, 2010. 21, 22, 23, 51

[116] Paul Ohm. Sensitive Information. *Southern California Law Review*, 88, pages 1125–1180, 2015. 25, 26, 51, 56

[117] Richard B. Parker. A Definition of Privacy. *Rutgers Law Review*, 27, page 275, 1973. 52

[118] Siani Pearson and Thomas Sander. A decision support system for privacy compliance. In *Threats, Countermeasures, and Advances in Applied Information Security, Information Science Reference, IGI Global*, pages 158–180. IGI Global, 2012. DOI: 10.4018/978-1-4666-0978-5.ch008. 1, 83

[119] Benny Pinkas. Cryptographic Techniques for Privacy-Preserving Data Mining. *ACM SIGKDD Explorations Newsletter*, 4(2), pages 12–19, 2002. DOI: 10.1145/772862.772865. 74

[120] Jules Polonetsky, Omer Tene, and Joseph Jerome. Benefit-risk Analysis for Big Data Projects, 2014. Future of Privacy Forum. xiii, 23

[121] Richard A. Posner. Privacy, Surveillance, and Law. *The University of Chicago Law Review*, pages 245–260, 2008. 52

[122] Elias Leake Quinn. Smart Metering and Privacy: Existing Laws and Competing Policies. *Available at SSRN 1462285*, 2009. DOI: 10.2139/ssrn.1462285. 13, 59

[123] S. Raj Rajagopalan, Lalitha Sankar, Soheil Mohajer, and H. Vincent Poor. Smart Meter Privacy: A Utility-Privacy Framework. In *IEEE International Conference on Smart Grid Communications (SmartGridComm)*, pages 190–195. IEEE, 2011. DOI: 10.1109/smartgridcomm.2011.6102315. 79

[124] Joel R. Reidenberg. Privacy Wrongs in Search of Remedies. *Hastings Law Journal*, 54, pages 877–900, 2002. DOI: 10.2139/ssrn.434585. 45, 46

[125] Alfredo Rial and George Danezis. Privacy-Preserving Smart Metering. In *Proc. of the 10th Annual ACM Workshop on Privacy in the Electronic Society*, pages 49–60. ACM, 2011. DOI: 10.1145/2046556.2046564. 79

[126] Cristina Rottondi, Giacomo Verticale, and Christopher Krauss. Distributed Privacy-Preserving Aggregation of Metering Data in Smart Grids. *IEEE Journal on Selected Areas in Communications*, 31(7), pages 1342–1354, 2013. DOI: 10.1109/jsac.2013.130716. 79

[127] Antoinette Rouvroy and Yves Poullet. The Right to Informational Self-determination and the Value of Self-development: Reassessing the Importance of Privacy for Democracy. In *Reinventing Data Protection: Proc. of the International Conference*, pages 45–76. Springer, 2009. DOI: 10.1007/978-1-4020-9498-9_2. 55

[128] Ira Rubinstein and Woodrow Hartzog. Anonymization and Risk. *Available at SSRN 2646185*, pages 1–54, 2015. xiii, 23

[129] Sushmita Ruj, Milos Stojmenovic, and Amiya Nayak. Privacy Preserving Access Control with Authentication for Securing Data in Clouds. In *12th IEEE/ACM International Symposium on Cluster, Cloud and Grid Computing (CCGrid)*, pages 556–563. IEEE, 2012. DOI: 10.1109/ccgrid.2012.92. 74

[130] Patricia Sánchez Abril. Recasting Privacy Torts in a Spaceless World. *Harvard Journal of Law and Technology*, 21, pages 1–47, 2007. 51

[131] Bruce Schneier. A Taxonomy of Social Networking Data. *IEEE Security and Privacy*, 8(4), page 88, 2010. DOI: 10.1109/msp.2010.118. 26

[132] Paul M. Schwartz. Privacy and Democracy in Cyberspace. *Vanderbilt Law Review*, 52, pages 1607–1702, 1999. DOI: 10.2139/ssrn.205449. 53, 54

[133] Paul M. Schwartz. Information Privacy in the Cloud. *University of Pennsylvania Law Review*, 161, pages 1623–1662, 2012. 37

[134] Paul M. Schwartz and Daniel J. Solove. The PII Problem: Privacy and a New Concept of Personally Identifiable Information. *New York University Law Review*, 86, pages 1814–1894, 2011. 4, 20, 22, 26, 51, 52, 53

[135] Paul M. Schwartz and Daniel J. Solove. Reconciling Personal Information in the United States and European Union. *California Law Review*, 102, pages 877–916, 2014. DOI: 10.2139/ssrn.2271442. 4, 20, 21, 25

[136] Andrew B. Serwin. Privacy 3.0—The Principle of Proportionality. *University of Michigan Journal of Law Reform*, 42(4), pages 869–961, 2009. DOI: 10.2139/ssrn.1089513. 25, 26

[137] Daniel J. Solove. Privacy and Power: Computer Databases and Metaphors for Information Privacy. *Stanford Law Review*, pages 1393–1462, 2001. DOI: 10.2307/1229546. 53

[138] Daniel J. Solove. Conceptualizing Privacy. *California Law Review*, pages 1087–1155, 2002. DOI: 10.2307/3481326. 52

[139] Daniel J. Solove. Identity Theft, Privacy, and the Architecture of Vulnerability. *Hastings Law Journal*, 54, pages 1227–1273, 2002. DOI: 10.2139/ssrn.416740. 54

[140] Daniel J. Solove. A Taxonomy of Privacy. *University of Pennsylvania Law Review*, pages 477–564, 2006. DOI: 10.2307/40041279. 7, 35, 45, 47, 51, 52, 53, 54

[141] Daniel J. Solove. 'I've Got Nothing to Hide' and Other Misunderstandings of Privacy. *San Diego Law Review*, 44, pages 745–772, 2007. 51, 54

[142] Latanya Sweeney. Uniqueness of Simple Demographics in the U.S. Population. Technical report, Carnegie Mellon University, 2000. 22

[143] Latanya Sweeney. k-anonymity: A Model for Protecting Privacy. *International Journal of Uncertainty, Fuzziness and Knowledge-Based Systems*, 10(05), pages 557–570, 2002. DOI: 10.1142/s0218488502001648. 74

[144] David Tancock, Siani Pearson, and Andrew Charlesworth. A Privacy Impact Assessment Tool for Cloud Computing. In *Privacy and Security for Cloud Computing*, pages 73–123. Springer, 2013. DOI: 10.1007/978-1-4471-4189-1_3. 1, 83

[145] Adam Thierer. Privacy, Security, and Human Dignity in the Dgital Age: The Pursuit of Privacy in a World Where Information Control Is Failing. *Harvard Journal of Law and Public Policy*, 36, pages 409–1245, 2013. 51

[146] United States. Children's Online Privacy Protection Act of 1998, 15 U.S.C. 6501–6508.

[147] United States. Gramm-Leach-Bliley Act or Financial Services Modernization Act of 1999 enacted by the 106th United States Congress.

[148] United States. Health Information Portability and Accountability Act of 1996 enacted by the 104th United States Congress.

[149] United States. Song-Beverly Credit Card Act of 1971.

[150] United States. Summary of the HIPPA Privacy Rule. http://www.hhs.gov/ocr/privacy/hipaa/understanding/summary/privacysummary.pdf. Accessed: 2015-10-01.

[151] United States. Video Privacy Protection Act of 1998, enacted by the 100th United States Congress.

[152] United States Court of Appeals, 7th Circuit. *Joan W. v. City of Chicago, 771 F.2d 1020.* 1985. 55

[153] United States Department of Homeland Security. Handbook for Safeguarding Sensitive Personally Identifiable Information, 2012. 24

[154] United States Supreme Court. *Doe v. Chao, 540 U.S. 614, 124 S. Ct. 1204, 157 L. Ed. 2d 1122.* 2004. 53, 55

[155] Niko Vidgren, Keijo Haataja, Jose Luis Patino-Andres, Juan Jose Ramirez-Sanchis, and Pekka Toivanen. Security Threats in ZigBee-enabled Systems: Vulnerability Evaluation, Practical Experiments, Countermeasures, and Lessons Learned. In *Proc. of the 46th Hawaii International Conference on System Sciences (HICSS)*, pages 5132–5138. IEEE, 2013. DOI: 10.1109/hicss.2013.475. 17

[156] Alexander E. Voiskounsky and Olga V. Smyslova. Flow-based Model of Computer Hackers' Motivation. *CyberPsychology and Behavior*, 6(2), pages 171–180, 2003. DOI: 10.1089/109493103321640365. 42

[157] Zhiyu Wan, Yevgeniy Vorobeychik, Weiyi Xia, Ellen Wright Clayton, Murat Kantarcioglu, Ranjit Ganta, Raymond Heatherly, and Bradley A. Malin. A Game Theoretic Framework for Analyzing Re-identification Risk. *PloS One*, 10(3):e0120592, 2015. DOI: 10.1371/journal.pone.0120592. 41

[158] Samuel D. Warren and Louis D. Brandeis. The Right to Privacy. *Harvard Law Review*, pages 193–220, 1890. DOI: 10.2307/1321160. 52, 54

[159] K. T. Weaver. A Perspective on How Smart Meters Invade Individual Privacy. https://skyvisionsolutions.files.wordpress.com/2014/08/utility-smart-meters-invade-privacy-22-aug-2014.pdf, 2014. Accessed: 2015-12-31. 13

[160] David Wright. The State of the Art in Privacy Impact Assessment. *Computer Law and Security Review*, 28(1), pages 54–61, 2012. DOI: 10.1016/j.clsr.2011.11.007. xiv, 1, 65

[161] David Wright. Making Privacy Impact Assessment More Effective. *The Information Society*, 29(5), pages 307–315, 2013. DOI: 10.1080/01972243.2013.825687. xiv, 69, 70

[162] David Wright and Paul De Hert. Introduction to Privacy Impact Assessment. In *Privacy Impact Assessment*, pages 3–32. Springer, 2012. DOI: 10.1007/978-94-007-2543-0_1. 63

[163] David Wright and Paul De Hert. *Privacy Impact Assessment*. Springer, 2012. DOI: 10.1007/978-94-007-2543-0. xiv, 1

[164] David Wright, Rachel Finn, and Rowena Rodrigues. A Comparative Analysis of Privacy Impact Assessment in Six Countries. *Journal of Contemporary European Research*, 9(1), 2013. 1

[165] Felix T. Wu. Defining Privacy and Utility in Data Sets. *University of Colorado Law Review*, 84, pages 1117–1257, 2013. DOI: 10.2139/ssrn.2031808. 21, 22, 23, 41, 43, 57

[166] Kim Wuyts. Privacy Threats in Software Architectures. *Doctoral thesis (KU Leuven)*, 2014. 12, 72, 74

[167] Jane Yakowitz. Tragedy of the Data Commons. *Harvard Journal of Law and Technology*, 25, pages 1–67, 2011. DOI: 10.2139/ssrn.1789749. 22, 23

[168] Lei Yang, Xu Chen, Junshan Zhang, and H. Vincent Poor. Cost-Effective and Privacy-Preserving Energy Management for Smart Meters. *IEEE Transactions on Smart Grid*, 6(1), pages 486–495, 2015. DOI: 10.1109/tsg.2014.2343611. 79

[169] Rani Yesudas and Roger Clarke. A Framework for Risk Analysis in Smart Grid. In *Critical Information Infrastructures Security*, pages 84–95. Springer, 2013. DOI: 10.1007/978-3-319-03964-0_8. 1

[170] Tobias Zillner and Sebastian Strobl. Zigbee Exploited-The Good, the Bad and the Ugly. *Black Hat USA*, 2015. 17

[171] Harald Zwingelberg and Marit Hansen. Privacy Protection Goals and Their Implications for eID Systems. In *Privacy and Identity Management for Life*, pages 245–260. Springer, 2012. DOI: 10.1007/978-3-642-31668-5_19. 26, 29

Authors' Biographies

SOURYA JOYEE DE

Sourya Joyee De received her Bachelor of Engineering degree in Information Technology from Bengal Engineering and Science University, Shibpur, India, in 2009 and became a Fellow of the Indian Institute of Management Calcutta (equivalent to Ph.D.) in December 2014. Thereafter, she was a Visiting Scientist at the R.C. Bose Centre for Cryptology & Security, Indian Statistical Institute, Kolkata. Since July 2015, she is an Inria post-doctoral researcher in the PRIVATICS research group and CITI laboratory in Lyon (France). Her research interests include privacy, security and applied cryptography.

DANIEL LE MÉTAYER

Daniel Le Métayer received a Ph.D. in computer science from the University of Rennes in 1984. He is a Senior Researcher ("Directeur de Recherche") with Inria and member of the PRIVATICS research group and CITI laboratory in Lyon (France). His research interests include privacy risk analysis, privacy by design, accountability and more generally the interactions between computer science and law.